A TV-DXers Handbook

IN PREPARATION

BP195   An Introduction to Communications and Direct Broadcast Satellites

A TV-DXers Handbook

by
R. Bunney

BERNARD BABANI (publishing) LTD
THE GRAMPIANS
SHEPHERDS BUSH ROAD
LONDON W6 7NF
ENGLAND

WARNING

Many television receivers have a live chassis and all have high voltages on certain components. Never work on, or make adjustments to a television receiver that is plugged into the mains unless you are certain that you know what you are doing.

Mention is made in the text of Sunspots. The Sun must never be viewed directly with a telescope or binoculars since serious injury to the eyes can result. Attempts at observing Sunspot activity should only be made by projecting the Sun onto a white card.

PLEASE NOTE

Although every care has been taken with the production of this book to ensure that any projects, designs, modifications and/or programs etc. contained herewith, operate in a correct and safe manner and also that any components specified are normally available in Great Britain, the Publishers do not accept responsibility in any way for the failure, including fault in design, of any project, design, modification or program to work correctly or to cause damage to any other equipment that it may be connected to or used in conjunction with, or in respect of any other damage or injury that may be so caused, nor do the Publishers accept responsibility in any way for the failure to obtain specified components.

Notice is also given that if equipment that is still under warranty is modified in any way or used or connected with home-built equipment then that warranty may be void.

This book is based on material originally published in Book No. BP52 *Long Distance Television Reception (TV-DX) for the Enthusiast.* © 1978, © 1979 Bernard Babani (publishing) Ltd.

© 1986 BERNARD BABANI (publishing) LTD

First Published — October 1986

British Library Cataloguing in Publication Data:
Bunney, R.
A TV-DXers Handbook. — (BP.176)
1. Direct broadcast satellite television ——Equipment and supplies
I. Title
621.388'5   TK6677

ISBN 0 85934 150 X

Printed and Bound by The Guernsey Press Co. Ltd, Channel Islands

PREFACE

Unlike its counterpart Short Wave radio, the art of long distance television reception had by its very specialised and technical nature remained an activity with a very small following until recent years. In the early 1960's the magazine 'Practical Television' first published a regular column intended for exponents of this hobby, edited by a true enthusiast, Charles Rafarel. Under Charles' inspired writing the hobby expanded into a considerable interest and in 1971 plans were made for a descriptive pamphlet covering all aspects of long distance television reception. Unfortunately Charles died before the project was completed.

IPC Magazines invited this author to continue the monthly column and over the past fifteen years the following has increased still further and continues to attract more enthusiasts each month. Long distance television reception (TV-DX) is a hobby that requires a degree of technical knowledge and competence, a hobby that can still allow a degree of original research and experimentation.

Between 1972 and 1976 there were published three editions of the 'Long Distance Television' booklet, presenting the basic theory and practical aspects of the hobby to both experienced and would-be enthusiasts. There has been considerable technical development since the 3rd edition of the 'Long Distance Television' booklet and quite dramatic advances are likely to occur in the next decade particularly with reception techniques. I am grateful therefore to Bernard Babani (publishing) Ltd for publishing an enlarged and updated volume presenting both established and new operational methods and practice.

This volume first appeared in late 1978 and in the first 18 months of its life changes within the broadcasting field merited an updated and expanded 2nd edition. With an increasing enthusiasm for DX-TV as a hobby, the 2nd edition outran supplies and a revised 3rd edition has now been published. By the end of 1985 there were over one dozen Ku (11/12 GHz) downlink cable TV programme channels available in Europe from various geosynchronous satellites, allowing reception by home terminals on relatively small dishes. The C band (3.65–4.2 GHz) satellite spectrum enjoys great popularity in the Americas with a profusion of downlinking satellite channels – C band in Europe unfortunately has limited scope at this time for experimental reception. Consequently the satellite section has been enlarged to encompass further generalised information since the coming decade direct to home transmissions will perhaps herald the most dramatic changes in the broadcasting field, both from a technical and political viewpoint.

By January 1985 all UK/Eire System A 405 line and French System E 819 line transmissions had ceased. The UK is re-engineering Bands 1/3 for mobile radio (PMR), amateur and other services whilst the French have opted for a 4th programme channel at Band 1/3 using System L and with limited PMR in Band 3 on frequencies away from local TV channels. At the time of writing the new French service (Canal Plus) is in part scrambled, the subscriber renting a decoder to resolve normal picture and sound from this service. With the advent of independent commercial TV in France in early 1986, Canal Plus scrambling periods are likely to decrease or even cease. In other European countries there is a trend away from Band 1 TV transmission and in coming years a decreasing number of transmitters/countries will be operational in Band 1. WARC '79 allocated further spectrum at the high frequency ends of both Band 3 and Band 5 to provide additional TV channels and the Band 2 VHF sound radio channels will be increased and eventually taking over the complete 88–108 MHz spectrum, now in part occupied by various utilities for communication purposes. The full Band 2 spectrum will be available for broadcasting in the UK by 1990. East European broadcasters now using the 68–73 MHz FM band are also likely to slowly migrate to the 88–108 MHz band in the coming decade.

A further development in terrestrial broadcasting is the use of the 12 GHz band for 'fill-in' relays into very small pockets of difficult reception. This technique is currently being exploited by Japan particularly in built up areas of dense population where a single large building may shadow a very localised area, the transmitter often being sited atop the obstruction itself! Stereo sound is also being used on a regular (daily) basis for TV programming by NHK (Japan), South Korea, and ZDF (West Germany); several other countries are now upgrading network transmission facilities for stereo – currently stereo transmissions on an experimental basis are being carried out in several other countries as well.

All the units and devices described within these pages have been designed and used by active enthusiasts. Often considerable ingenuity and thought has gone into the development of such units in surmounting individual problems.

Finally, my thanks are due to the many friends that have co-operated and assisted with the production of this volume – without whose help much of the information would not have been available.

Roger Bunney – October 1986

ACKNOWLEDGEMENTS

The author wishes to thank the following organisations and individuals for their assistance and co-operation in the preparation of this volume.

British Broadcasting Corporation

Independent Broadcasting Authority

'Television', IPC Magazines Ltd, London
— particularly for their permission to reproduce material originally published in 'Television'

Antiference Ltd, Aylesbury

British Amateur Television Club (BATC)

Harrison Electronics Ltd, March, Cambs.

Jaybeam Ltd, Northampton

Space Communications (SAT-TEL) Ltd, Northampton

Aerial Techniques, Poole

Thorn-EMI-Ferguson Ltd

Wolsey Electronics Ltd, Pontypridd

Paul Barton

Alan Beech

Steve Birkill

Robin Crossley

Robert Copeman

Alan Damper

Cliff Dykes

Graham Deaves

Nick Harrold

Dave Lauder

Anthony Mann

Ryn Muntjewerff

Alan Latham

Chris Wilson

CONTENTS

INTRODUCTION

As most television viewers will be aware, only a limited number of stations are available to them at reasonable strengths in their particular area. Viewers in the United Kingdom normally have available 4 programme channels transmitted within a UHF channel grouping from a common transmitting site. Such a transmitting site will be a high powered 'main' transmitter usually located upon elevated ground, or a low powered relay serving a restricted area that is shielded from the main transmitter and hence requiring an improved signal field strength. Examples of both a main and relay transmitters are shown in the accompanying photographs. Tuning onto other channels will often reveal somewhat weaker signals from adjoining transmission areas. At some favourable high locations a number of alternative programmes may be available at fair signal strengths, thus enthusing the viewer to erect suitable aerials to enable reception of stronger and more consistent signals.

Television signals are transmitted at VHF (Very High Frequency) or UHF (Ultra High Frequency). Such frequencies must be used for television due to the extremely wide bandwidths required to transmit high definition vision and sound information. Due to the use of VHF and UHF, television transmissions are limited to the area surrounding the transmitter, extending to the optical horizon and a little beyond at lower field strengths. The depth of the latter area will depend upon a number of factors, the main one being the frequency involved, e.g. a greater area for a transmitter operating at 50 MHz than say a transmitter operating at 800 MHz. To provide as large a coverage area as possible from the transmitter, a high transmitting mast is used, with high gain aerials often in use to favour one direction in preference to another direction or area. The field strength delivered to a receiving site will therefore depend upon a number of factors: the frequency of the transmitter's effective radiating power (erp), the height of transmitting mast and the intervening terrain between the transmitter and receiving site. Thus at some distance beyond the optical horizon it would at first seem that distant signals would be too weak to be of any use in providing viewable pictures. However it is certainly possible to obtain reception of such transmissions at very considerable distances, often at high signal strengths.

With the advent of the communications satellite and direct satellite-to-home TV transmissions new

Crystal Palace, London, transmitting site, a BBC/IBA main station at 1000 kw erp., Group A. The mast is 211 metres high (to transmitting array centre)

A typical small BBC/IBA relay at Alton, Hampshire operating at 10 watts in Group C/D

1

techniques in signal reception and demodulation are being evolved. The successful ATS-6 experiment with educational broadcasts to the Indian sub-continent show that it is possible to receive and display TV pictures in areas some thousands of miles from the target area and on modified domestic apparatus.

In 1975/76 the ATS-6 (SITE) experiment allowed early DBS (direct broadcasting by satellite) reception from a NASA satellite at 35°E (carrying Indian TV programming) and signals were received by DX enthusiasts. At the present time the EKRAN satellite provides UHF DBS of the Russian 1st TV programme service, and although intended for Northern USSR it is receivable over much of the Earth's surface that is in sight of its 99°E orbital slot. However this reception may well be of indifferent quality when off of boresight. Reception of 4 GHz TV satellite down-links (intended generally in a telecommunications capacity) is available with suitable equipment (a 2 m dish as a minimum) in Europe, including the Russian 1st programme via GORIZONT 7 satellite at 14°W (3.675 GHz).

North America has available many dozens of downlink TV channels from a variety of DOMSATs (now fast approaching a congestion situation), with a vast array of relatively inexpensive commercial equipment available on the domestic market. Ku band will be the norm for European DBS and current-ly several satellites provide TV programme downlinks in the 10.9–12.5 GHz spectrum (intended mainly for cable companies).

The mechanism by which these signals are propag-ated and received will be discussed later but initially it is necessary to detail the various television trans-mission systems at present in use throughout the world.

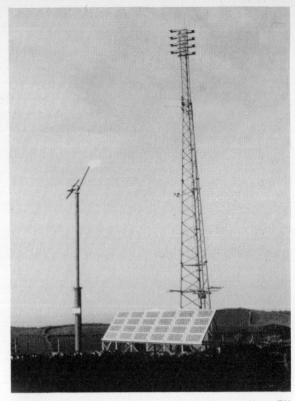

Bossiney Group C/D relay in West Cornwall at 7½ watts output. This IBA ecological relay obtains its power from Solar Panels and a wind generator. Back-up mains power is available though the relay itself has operated since opening on Solar/wind energy

International Transmission Standards

System	Line No.	Overall channel bandwidth (MHz)	Vision bandwidth (MHz)	Sound/vision spacing (MHz)	Vision modu-lation	Sound modu-lation	Areas in use
A	405	5	3	−3.5	+	AM	
B	625	7	5	+5.5	−	FM	Western Europe, parts of Africa, Middle East, India, Far East, Australasia (VHF)
C	625	7	5	+5.5	+	AM	
D	625	8	6	+6.5	−	FM	Eastern Europe, USSR, China (VHF/UHF)
E	819	14	10	±11.15	+	AM	
F	819	7	5	+5.5	+	AM	
G/H	625	8	5	+5.5	−	FM	Western Europe (UHF), System H has a 1.25 MHz vestigal sideband used in Belgium (UHF)
I	625	8	5.5	+6.0	−	FM	UK (UHF), Eire (VHF/UHF), Republic of South Africa (VHF/UHF)
K	625	8	6	+6.5	−	FM	French Territories overseas.
L	625	8	6	+6.5	+	AM	France, Luxembourg.
M	525	6	4.2	+4.5	−	FM	North & South America, Caribbean, parts of Pacific, Far East, US Forces broadcasting (AFRTS), Japan.

N.B.: Systems A, C, E, F are no longer in use but are included in this table for historical and reference purposes, the various channel/frequency allocations for Systems A and E are included in later pages of this volume.

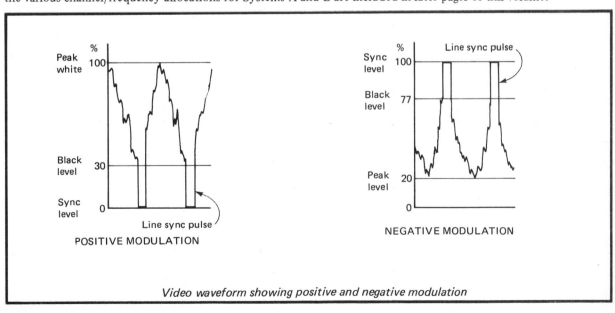

Video waveform showing positive and negative modulation

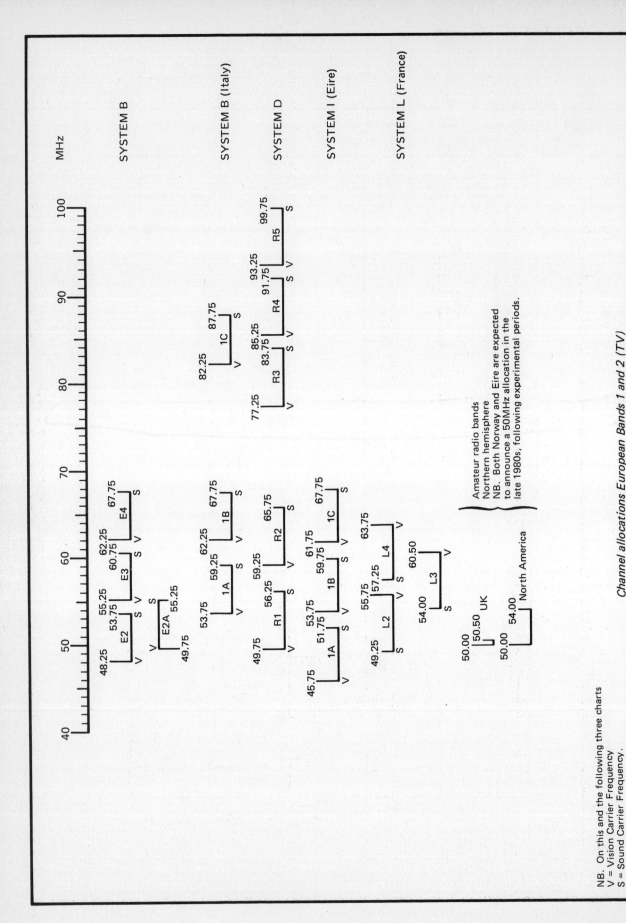

Channel allocations European Bands 1 and 2 (TV)

NB. On this and the following three charts
V = Vision Carrier Frequency
S = Sound Carrier Frequency.

4

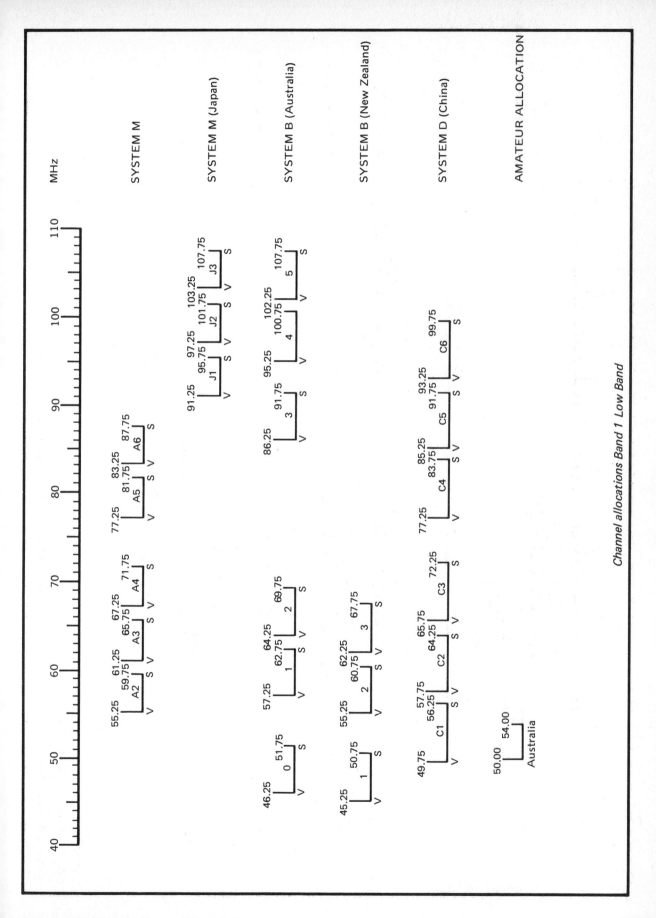

Channel allocations Band 1 Low Band

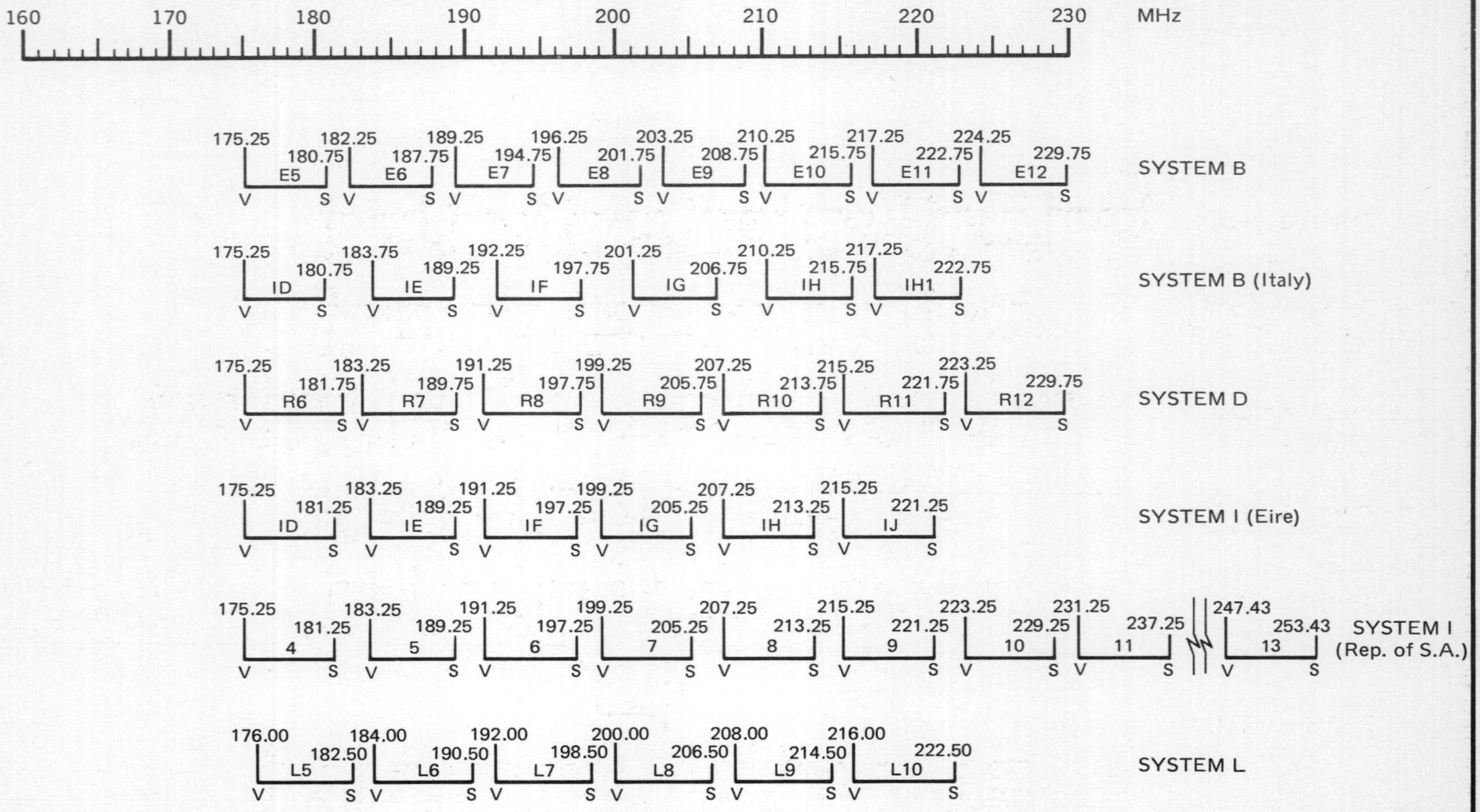

MHz

160 170 180 190 200 210 220 230

SYSTEM B
E5 — V 175.25 / S 180.75
E6 — V 182.25 / S 187.75
E7 — V 189.25 / S 194.75
E8 — V 196.25 / S 201.75
E9 — V 203.25 / S 208.75
E10 — V 210.25 / S 215.75
E11 — V 217.25 / S 222.75
E12 — V 224.25 / S 229.75

SYSTEM B (Italy)
ID — V 175.25 / S 180.75
IE — V 183.75 / S 189.25
IF — V 192.25 / S 197.75
IG — V 201.25 / S 206.75
IH — V 210.25 / S 215.75
IH1 — V 217.25 / S 222.75

SYSTEM D
R6 — V 175.25 / S 181.75
R7 — V 183.25 / S 189.75
R8 — V 191.25 / S 197.75
R9 — V 199.25 / S 205.75
R10 — V 207.25 / S 213.75
R11 — V 215.25 / S 221.75
R12 — V 223.25 / S 229.75

SYSTEM I (Eire)
ID — V 175.25 / S 181.25
IE — V 183.25 / S 189.25
IF — V 191.25 / S 197.25
IG — V 199.25 / S 205.25
IH — V 207.25 / S 213.25
IJ — V 215.25 / S 221.25

SYSTEM I (Rep. of S.A.)
4 — V 175.25 / S 181.25
5 — V 183.25 / S 189.25
6 — V 191.25 / S 197.25
7 — V 199.25 / S 205.25
8 — V 207.25 / S 213.25
9 — V 215.25 / S 221.25
10 — V 223.25 / S 229.25
11 — V 231.25 / S 237.25
13 — V 247.43 / S 253.43

SYSTEM L
L5 — V 176.00 / S 182.50
L6 — V 184.00 / S 190.50
L7 — V 192.00 / S 198.50
L8 — V 200.00 / S 206.50
L9 — V 208.00 / S 214.50
L10 — V 216.00 / S 222.50

Channel allocations Band 3

6

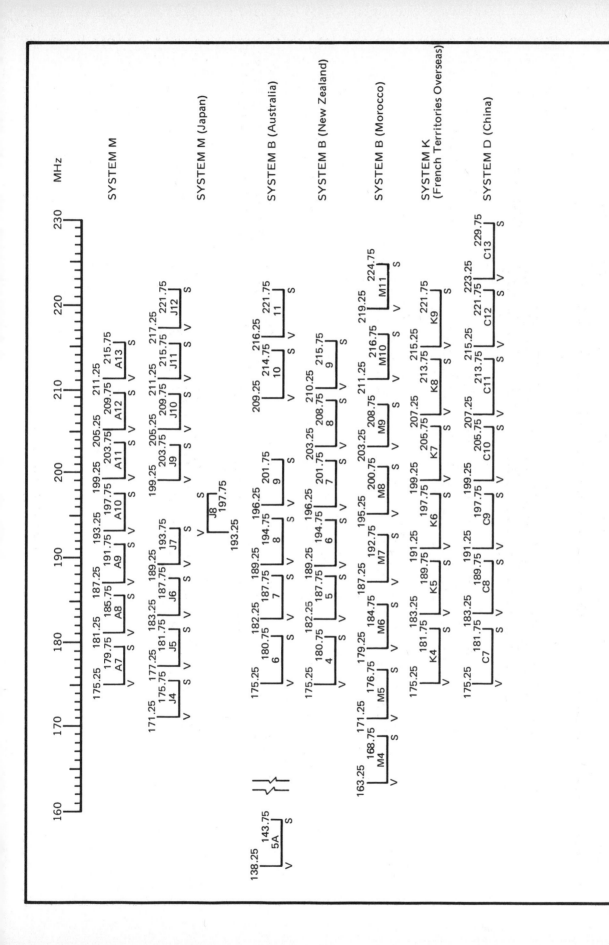

Channel allocations Band 3 High Band

Channel Allocations Bands 4 and 5 — Systems D, G, H, I, K, L
Vision Carrier Frequencies (MHz)
(The Sound Carrier is spaced from the Vision Carrier by the following:

Systems G, H	+5.5 MHz
Systems I	+6.0 MHz
Systems D, K, L	+6.5 MHz)

21	471.25	31	551.25	41	631.25	51	711.25	61	791.25
22	479.25	32	559.25	42	639.25	52	719.25	62	799.25
23	487.25	33	567.25	43	647.25	53	727.25	63	807.25
24	495.25	34	575.25	44	655.25	54	735.25	64	815.25
25	503.25	35	583.25	45	663.25	55	743.25	65	823.25
26	511.25	36	591.25	46	671.25	56	751.25	66	831.25
27	519.25	37	599.25	47	679.25	57	759.25	67	839.25
28	527.25	38	607.25	48	687.25	58	767.25	68	847.25
29	535.25	39	615.25	49	695.25	59	775.25		
30	543.25	40	623.25	50	703.25	60	783.25		

Channel Allocations Bands 4 and 5 — System M
Vision Carrier Frequencies (MHz)
(The Sound Carrier is spaced at +4.5 MHz)

A14	471.25	A28	555.25	A42	639.25	A56	723.25	A70	807.25
A15	477.25	A29	561.25	A43	645.25	A57	729.25	A71	813.25
A16	483.25	A30	567.25	A44	651.25	A58	735.25	A72	819.25
A17	489.25	A31	573.25	A45	657.25	A59	741.25	A73	825.25
A18	495.25	A32	579.25	A46	663.25	A60	747.25	A74	831.25
A19	501.25	A33	585.25	A47	669.25	A61	753.25	A75	837.25
A20	507.25	A34	591.25	A48	675.25	A62	759.25	A76	843.25
A21	513.25	A35	597.25	A49	681.25	A63	765.25	A77	849.25
A22	519.25	A36	603.25	A50	687.25	A64	771.25	A78	855.25
A23	525.25	A37	609.25	A51	693.25	A65	777.25	A79	861.25
A24	531.25	A38	615.25	A52	699.25	A66	783.25	A80	867.25
A25	537.25	A39	621.25	A53	705.25	A67	789.25	A81	873.25
A26	543.25	A40	627.25	A54	711.25	A68	795.25	A82	879.25
A27	549.25	A41	633.25	A55	717.25	A69	801.25	A83	885.25

Channel Allocations Band 5 — System M — Japan only
Vision Carrier Frequencies (MHz)
(The Sound Carrier is spaced at +4.5 MHz)

J13	471.25	J23	531.25	J33	591.25	J43	651.25	J53	711.25
J14	477.25	J24	537.25	J34	597.25	J44	657.25	J54	717.25
J15	483.25	J25	543.25	J35	603.25	J45	663.25	J55	723.25
J16	489.25	J26	549.25	J36	609.25	J46	669.25	J56	729.25
J17	495.25	J27	555.25	J37	615.25	J47	675.25	J57	735.25
J18	501.25	J28	561.25	J38	621.25	J48	681.25	J58	741.25
J19	507.25	J29	567.25	J39	627.25	J49	687.25	J59	747.25
J20	513.25	J30	573.25	J40	633.25	J50	693.25	J60	753.25
J21	519.25	J31	579.25	J41	639.25	J51	699.25	J61	759.25
J22	525.25	J32	585.25	J42	645.25	J52	705.25	J62	765.25

Channel Allocations for System A and System E

System A (405 lines)			System E (819 lines)		
Channel	Sound (MHz)	Vision (MHz)	Channel	Sound (MHz)	Vision (MHz)
B1	41.50	45.00	F2	41.25	52.40
B2	48.25	51.75	F4	54.40	65.55
B3	53.25	56.75	F5	175.15	164.00
B4	58.25	61.75	F6	162.25	173.40
B5	63.25	66.75	F7	188.30	177.15
B6	176.25	179.75	F8	175.40	186.55
B7	181.25	184.75	F8a	174.10	185.25
B8	186.25	189.75	F9	201.45	190.30
B9	191.25	194.75	F10	188.55	199.70
B10	196.25	199.75	F11	214.60	203.45
B11	201.25	204.75	F12	201.70	212.85
B12	206.26	209.75			
B13	211.25	214.75			

Australian UHF TV Channel Numbers and Frequency Limits
(Courtesy of ABC)

BAND IV

Channel 28	526–533 MHz	Channel 29	533–540 MHz	Channel 30	540–547 MHz
Channel 31	547–554 MHz	Channel 32	554–561 MHz	Channel 33	561–568 MHz
Channel 34	568–575 MHz	Channel 35	575–582 MHz		

BAND V

Channel 39	603–610 MHz	Channel 40	610–617 MHz	Channel 41	617–624 MHz
Channel 42	624–631 MHz	Channel 43	631–638 MHz	Channel 44	638–645 MHz
Channel 45	645–652 MHz	Channel 46	652–659 MHz	Channel 47	659–666 MHz
Channel 48	666–673 MHz	Channel 49	673–680 MHz	Channel 50	680–687 MHz
Channel 51	687–694 MHz	Channel 52	694–701 MHz	Channel 53	701–708 MHz
Channel 54	708–715 MHz	Channel 55	715–722 MHz	Channel 56	722–729 MHz
Channel 57	729–736 MHz	Channel 58	736–743 MHz	Channel 59	743–750 MHz
Channel 60	750–757 MHz	Channel 61	757–764 MHz	Channel 62	764–771 MHz
Channel 63	771–778 MHz	Channel 64	778–785 MHz	Channel 65	785–792 MHz
Channel 66	792–799 MHz	Channel 67	799–806 MHz	Channel 68	806–813 MHz
Channel 69	813–820 MHz				

		Overall Channel Bandwidth (MHz)	Vision Carrier (MHz)
	S 2	111 — 118	Note 1)
	S 3	118 — 125	,,
	S 4	125 — 132	Note 1)
	S 5	132 — 139	,,
Lowband channels	S 6	139 — 146	140,25
	S 7	146 — 153	147,25
	S 8	153 — 160	154,25
	S 9	160 — 167	161,25
	S10	167 — 174	168,25
Broadcast Band 3 channels 174—230 MHz			
Midband channels	S11	230 — 237	231,25
	S12	237 — 244	238,25
	S13	244 — 251	245,25
	S14	251 — 258	252,25
	S15	258 — 265	259,25
	S16	265 — 272	266,25
	S17	272 — 279	273,25
Pilot channels	S18	279 — 286	280,25
	S19	286 — 293	287,25
	S20	293 — 300	294,25
Channels	S21	302 — 310	303,25
	S22	310 — 318	311,25
	S23	318 — 326	319,25
	S24	326 — 334	327,25
	S25	334 — 342	335,25
	S26	342 — 350	343,25
	S27	350 — 358	351,25
	S28	358 — 366	359,25
	S29	366 — 374	367,25
	S30	374 — 382	375,25
	S31	382 — 390	383,25
	S32	390 — 398	391,25
	S33	398 — 406	399,25
	S34	406 — 414	407,25
	S35	414 — 422	415,25
	S36	422 — 430	423,25
	S37	430 — 438	431,25

European Cable Channel Allocations

West European TV tuners are available covering cable allocations to either S20 or to S37 as detailed below. Many European manufactured receivers have them fitted as standard due to the high cable penetration in the Benelux/West Germany area (see footnote 3) Belgium.

Notes:
1) Wideband communications channels.
2) Channel S1 (104—111 MHz) in disuse as within Band 2 broadcast spectrum.
3) Belgium channels have variations to the above as follows: M1 to M10 = S1 to S10; U1 to U9 = S11 to S19; not in use S20 to S37.
   Belgium's S1 to S3 have vision carriers of 69.25, 76.25, 83.25 MHz respectively.

As mentioned in the introduction the normal service area from a high powered transmitter at VHF or UHF extends to and just beyond the optical horizon. Such reception within this area is termed 'direct' reception and is basically a 'line of sight' medium — one in which the receiving aerial can 'see' the transmitting aerial. Since we are interested in the more esoteric forms of signal propagation and over far greater distances than relatively near signal sources, direct signal propagation need not concern us here — at least in the terrestrial sense. Direct propagation does however have greater implications when discussing satellite transmission — covered later in this volume — and with various attempts at airborn transmissions. Television transmissions have already been successfully relayed from both moored balloons and circling aircraft.

Tropospheric

The service area from a television transmitter extends to just beyond the optical horizon, at that point signals start to fall off in strength rapidly. Viewers living in such a fringe area will have noticed that during certain conditions the signal improves considerably and possibly even noticing interference from another transmitter, displaying itself as line-pairing or even a floating picture. Such conditions are related to the prevailing state of the Troposphere. The Troposphere is that part of the Earth's atmosphere adjacent to the ground and extending to about 20,000 feet. When weather conditions become very settled, as with a slow moving high pressure system (Anti-Cyclone), Tropospheric propagation is likely to be enhanced and producing an extended fringe area. Often during the late Summer/Autumn months such a weather system can become virtually stationary over Western Europe. The daytime produces clear, cloudless skies, with a rapid fall in temperature at night. As the evening approaches following such a warm cloudless day, the upper air cools, as does the surface temperature, but at different rates. This produces a boundary or temperature gradient and hence the formation of an inversion layer. Under such conditions improved Tropospheric propagation will occur especially if fog forms. Fog is likely to form over the sea and coastal areas and to some extent inland. The improved reception conditions will be noticed as darkness falls, remaining until the following morning, when conditions again deteriorate as the Sun heats the lower Troposphere and disperses the fog. Reception is often favoured along a path parallel with the prevailing Isobar pattern rather than across the pattern. (Note. Isobars are lines joining equal points of pressure.) As the high pressure system moves away another effect — Tropospheric Ducting — often occurs. Signals are ducted along the trailing edge of the system over some considerable distance.

Tropospheric propagation — UHF ch.E34 Pajala, Sweden received in Holland at +1100 miles (1800 km) (RMU)

Tropospheric — UHF ch.E42 West German transmitter identification slide (RMU)

The upper air duct can be selective both in frequency and distance, often a distant transmitter is received, whereas a closer transmitter operating on the same frequency is by-passed. If a high pressure system is stationary for some considerable time upper air ducts can form at any time even during the daytime, when conventional Tropospheric signals tend to be less favourably propagated. A fast moving weather system can also produce ducts, either 'pushing' it in front or dragging it on the trailing edge.

In certain areas of the World, notably the Mediterranean and the Arabian Gulf, ducting conditions can become established for many months of the year and such as to allow regular reception of television signals at entertainment quality, and over distances of several hundreds of miles. Such conditions are normally established during the very hot settled Summer weather and can result in severe interference. The broadcasting authorities in the Arabian

Gulf are currently discussing an eventual move to UHF in the hope of reducing the problem to the existing TV services.

The characteristic signal both by conventional Tropospheric propagation and by ducting is a slow fading stable signal. At times selective fading may be

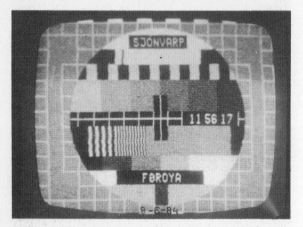

Enhanced Tropospheric propagation — Band 3 ch.E6 Faroe Islands received in Holland (RMU)

noted with the sound frequency fading independently of the vision and vice versa. Frequencies affected cover all those used for television transmission although Band 1 is less favourably propagated than that of Band 3 and UHF. Distances encountered can reach in excess of 1,000 miles for both VHF and UHF signals.

The photographs show typical enhanced Tropospheric reception, one of a slow fading noisy signal over a very long path. At times however both Band 3 and UHF Tropospheric signals can lift to very high levels as is illustrated in these three photographs, received at a TV-DXer's home in Holland.

Sporadic E

By means of Short Wave radio it is possible to transmit signals to distant countries and indeed around the world itself. Such communication is dependent upon a number of reflecting layers high above the Earth's surface known as the E, F1 and F2 layers. There is a fourth layer — the D layer — but this need not concern us here. The E layer lies at an approximate height of seventy-five miles, and under normal conditions reflects Short Wave signals, VHF and UHF signals passing straight through this layer and indeed the F layers and are lost in space. At certain times however, patches of the E layer become intensely ionised and reflect signals back to Earth at frequencies well into the VHF spectrum. During such conditions television transmissions in Bands 1 and 2, and very occasionally Band 3, are capable of being reflected, allowing reception at distances upwards of 500 miles.

The cause of Sporadic E ionisation is not exactly known but various theories have been presented as to its cause. These have included meteor shower ionisation, effects from electrical thunder storms, ionospheric winds producing E layer irregularities, effects from Sunspots and other solar activity and electrical currents flowing within the E layer. No conclusive theory has yet been formulated as to the origin of Sporadic E indeed there may be more than one cause. Attempts to connect the incidence of Sporadic E with the eleven year Sunspot cycle have proved fruitless — at least on a world wide scale. In early 1980 details of research were published suggesting that Sporadic E may originate as a result of ionisation from meteor ionisation and work continues in this specific field with the hope that the cause of intense Sporadic E ionisation may be established.

Although Sporadic E can occur at any time of the year, the most active period is during the Summer months, from early May to September and in some

Double hop multi-path Sporadic E — Syria ch.E3 received in Holland (RMU)

Double hop 'exotic' Sporadic E — Aramco TV, Dhahran, Saudi Arabia ch.E3 received in Finland (PPN)

years a small peak of activity has been noted in mid-Winter. The Sporadic E cloud itself may be small or widespread and is capable of movement of up to 250 m.p.h. This results in a changing length of signal skip path, with signals being received from consecutive transmitters, either close or more distant depending upon the direction of movements of the cloud. The length of a skip path varies between 500 – 1,400 miles approximately and at times double or even triple hop has been known to occur. The signals as received via Sporadic E can be extremely strong and range in strength over a few seconds from just detectable to overloading. Polarisation shift can be considerable often being completely random, although for the longer skip signals polarisation tends to remain in the original transmitted polarisation and together with a more stable signal not unlike a characteristic Tropospheric signal. For the shorter skip signals of up to 1,000 miles or so, signals can be reflected from more than one part of the Sporadic E

layer, resulting in multiple images and ghosting, with at times phase reversal and other effects. It does appear that at times part of the Sporadic E reflecting layer may form in a more vertical plane as often signals are noted arriving from up to 30° off the correct bearing for the transmitter. From year to year Sporadic E may tend to favour alternative directions and areas such as Sporadic E openings predominating particular stations or countries over that of other regions.

When very short skip Sporadic E is noticed — which will usually indicate intense ionisation patches within the E Layer, there is every possibility of E Layer back-scatter. An example of this phenomenon occurred in May 1980 when during an intense short skip Sporadic E opening the Gort, ch.IB in Eire was being received in the London area, signals on ch.E3 from Liege, Belgium were also received but from a Westerly direction.

Although the frequencies most likely to be pro-

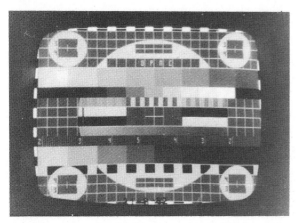

Sporadic E — the 0167 test card ch.R3 from the USSR (RMU)

Multi-hop Sporadic E. A very fine reception on ch.A2 showing station logo of TV-2 Guaiba, Porto Alegre, Brazil — received in Holland at 10,200 km (RMU)

Sporadic E — USSR, despite extensive networking regional variations such as local news can sometimes be received — this example shows the Volograd ch.R1 identification slide (RMU)

Band 3 Sporadic E reception, this of USSR ch.R8 in Band 3 from the Ukraine in Holland (RMU)

pagated are within Bands 1 and 2, on rare occasions signals have been noted at the low frequency end of Band 3. If very short skip is seen, i.e. under 500 miles in Band 1, then there is every possibility that the ionised area will be capable of reflecting a signal of much higher frequency — possibly a Band 3 channel — since a sharp reflection angle (short skip) favours lower frequencies, a shallower reflection angle from the same ionised cloud will favour a higher frequency: with a shallower reflection angle a single hop signal will come from a much greater distance.

Sporadic E — Rosario, Argentina ch.A3 received at Port Stanley, Falkland Islands

There is a tendency for Sporadic E to occur during spells of thundery weather in the Summer months especially if thunder storms are noted locally.

A related form of E Layer propagation is Auroral-E propagation. There is a characteristic 'flutter' to an Auroral-E signal which tends to occur towards the end of the 2nd phase of an Auroral event, generally late at night. As with an Aurora the tendency will be for Auroral-E signals to be received from a Northerly direction (from North East through North to North West).

In the Southern Hemisphere the Sporadic E season also occurs during the Summer period but some 6 months after the Northern Hemisphere, specifically from November onwards. Enthusiasts have noted a link with Trans Equatorial propagation which during the evening period can lead to reception of Korean and Chinese transmitters in Northern Australia.

The duration of Sporadic E signals can range from a few minutes to several hours, often at sustained high signal strengths. For the beginner with little experience of TV-DXing, Sporadic E is recommended for initial experiments, as spectacular results can be obtained with the minimum of equipment.

Meteor Shower/Scatter

Throughout the twenty-four hour period, as the Earth moves through space in orbit around the Sun, it encounters small particles of rock and dust. Such random particles, often no larger than ¼ inch in diameter, enter the various layers that surround the Earth and burn up, appearing as the well known 'Shooting Star'. In addition to the random particles, the Earth often encounters large areas of particles, themselves in orbit around the Sun. Such particles comprise what is known as a Meteor Shower occurring at regular times and periods and are consequently predictable.

When a particle enters the upper atmosphere it burns due to friction. As the particle burns a train of ionisation is produced, generally at the E layer height. If the ionisation density is sufficiently high it is able to reflect a signal at VHF that would normally pass through the E layer (except for Sporadic E as already discussed). Consequently an incident television signal is capable of being reflected up to distances approaching that of conventional Sporadic E propagation. A signal reflected by such meteor ionisation can vary in duration from fractions of a second up to five seconds for really intense ionised trails, and the signal strengths encountered also vary considerably from very weak and almost undetectable up to strong. A particle that enters the atmosphere at an extremely high speed will burn at a greater height than a slow moving particle which will burn at a lower height. Consequently a high velocity particle will tend to give a greater skip distance than that of a slower particle.

The best time for observing random meteors is the early morning period, when the velocity of the Earth relative to the velocity of the particles is greatest, although of course such phenomena can occur at any time of the day or night. The regular meteor showers can produce extremely good reflections of a fairly long duration due to the number of particles burning up at E layer height. The more important showers and approximate dates of arrival are listed below. The exact dates for any year may be found in various astronomical year books.

Quadrantids	early January
Lyrids	mid April
May Aquarids	early May
Cetids	mid May
Delta Aquarids	end July
Perseids	end July/mid August
Giacobinids	early October
Orionids	mid/late October
Taurids	early November
Leonids	mid November
Geminids	early/mid December
Ursids	mid/late December

Frequencies affected by such meteor scatter propagation tend to favour Band 1, although at certain times with extremely intense trails, instances of Band 3 signal reception can occur. Such signals often peak to levels similar to that in Band 1 although generally of shorter duration. The lower frequency channels in Band 3 tend to be more favourably received. It has been noted that if a Band 3 MS 'ping' is observed lower frequency signal 'pings' in Band 1 will follow some seconds later, the latter being of greater intensity and sustained over a longer period. It is therefore often possible to identify a weak Band 3 'ping' if the following Band 1 signal is stronger and of longer duration, this assumes of course that a similar test pattern or programme is seen. It goes without saying that equipment for successful meteor shower work needs to be of high gain and with extremely good synchronisation properties. As signals to some extent will tend to arrive from the E layer at an angle relative to the horizontal, a slight tilt upwards of the receiving aerial may be found to give an improvement, especially if a multi-element array is being used with an extremely narrow vertical acceptance angle.

F2 Layer

Solar activity has a cycle of approximately eleven years, during which time Sunspot activity rises to a peak and falls again to a low figure. When Sunspot activity increases, so do the reflecting capabilities of the various layers surrounding the Earth, enabling high frequencies to be used with Short Wave communications. The highest reflecting layer, the F2 layer — some 200 miles above the Earth during the Winter daytime, receives Ultra Violet radiation from the Sun, causing ionisation of the gasses within this layer. If Solar activity is sufficiently high the Ionisation Density is such to reflect signals at extremely high frequencies and into the lower VHF spectrum. At this point it may be worth mentioning that the incident signal entering the F2 layer is actually returned by a process of refraction but for simplicity the term reflection is used. At periods of

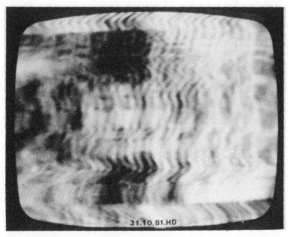

F2 Layer propagation — typical strong multi-path signal propagation — unidentified ch.E2 in Holland

high Solar activity the MUF (Maximum Usable Frequency) rises and the F2 layer is able to reflect signals over considerable distances; a maximum single hop can reach up to 2,500 miles. There is a variation in the height and formation of the F1 and F2 layers depending upon Solar activity, time of the year and whether day or night-time. Similarly there is a variation in the MUF between the Summer and Winter, being highest during the Winter day-time, caused by the less expanded state of the F2 layer, whereas in the Summer the F2 layer receives more

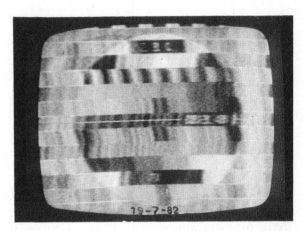

F2 Layer — relatively good quality though smearing test card from Zimbabwe Television ch.E2 (identification top 'ZBC', bottom 'TV'), seen in Holland (RMU)

heat and is in a state of greater expansion, resulting in a lower number of electrons per unit space.

Generally a signal path running North/South is more favourable than East/West and in most cases successful VHF propagation via the F2 layer will necessitate Noon between the transmitting and receiving points, in order to obtain the required MUF. Vision signals propagated via the F2 layer tend to suffer severe multiple images and smearing with phase reversal and associated effects. Frequencies affected will of course depend upon Solar activity and can be predicted quite accurately. An associated effect with high Solar activity is Trans Equatorial Skip sometimes known as Equatorial Spread F. Towards Sunset the two day-time F layers break up and merge to form one layer at approximately 250 miles high. As the F2 layer breaks up into small clouds, multiple reflections occur, as signals are scattered through the cloud region. Such reception occurs between points either side of the Equator, on a North/South path, usually limited to a region 40° either side of the Equator, but at times reaching well into the UK. It is sometimes possible to obtain signal reflection on an East/West path within a region 15° North/South of the

Equator. Signals, as with conventional F2 layer propagation, suffer with multiple images, smearing and with a characteristic flutter effect. Recent observation notes by radio amateurs suggest that Trans Equatorial Skip may occur during periods when Solar activity is low. Tests between Japan and Australia confirm that such propagation can be established within Band 1 and extending to 70 MHz during the evening period between 20.00 and 24.00 local time, generally the most favourable period for such conditions to be experienced are the Equinoxes (i.e. March/April and September/October).

Both F2 layer and Trans Equatorial Skip (TE) are dependent upon Solar activity and generally such activity needs to be very high before propgatation at lower VHF occurs. During both the 1956-8 and 1978-80 Sunspot maxima, the reception of Crystal Palace ch.B1, in the United Kingdom was common throughout the world and at times frequencies up to 62 MHz were being received across the North Atlantic.

The high level of Sunspot activity that reached a peak in late 1979/early 1980 gave record F2 activity into the VHF bands. Signals were received on ch.A2 and ch.A3 video (61.25 MHz) in the UK as were various UK 405 line transmissions noted in the USA on channels up to ch.B4 video and System B vision signals to ch.E4. Australian TV signals were received on several occasions in the UK on ch.A0 and in Australia BBC TV was relatively commonplace on both channels B1 and B2 with sound and vision. From a receiving site in the UK a typical sequence of F2 propagated signals would be distant ch.R1 signals from the USSR at 0800/0830 GMT and suffering

BBC1 on ch.B1 received in Perth, Australia via intense F2 Layer propagation in November 1979

characteristic multiple images and smearing. As the morning progressed so shorter distance signals would be noted until at Midday the closest hop signals at 3000 miles (Armenian SSR) were seen. African stations then appeared and after Midday North American TV transmitters on chs. A2 and rarely A3 arrived. Conditions during this period were such that inevitably several stations would be present at any one time making identification impossible. Optimum times for identification seemed to occur at the commencement of skip into a given area when perhaps only one signal would initially be present.

During very active periods a secondary effect of intense F2 propagation is F2 backscatter. An example of this phenomenon can occur from relatively close transmitters when a signal is reflected from the distant F2 layer back to the receiving site but from a seemingly incorrect direction. An example of this has been Czechoslovakian TV transmitters operating on ch.R1 being received in the South UK but the signal direction being the South West rather than the normal Easterly direction. The backscatter signals would be present during F2 openings giving rise to confusion with the multiplicity of signals at both F2 and Sporadic E distances.

Aurora

During periods of high Solar activity, there is a great possibility of a Solar Flare erupting upon the face of the Sun. When such an eruption occurs, charged particles are emitted from the Sun and spiral towards the Earth, taking about twenty-four hours for the journey. As the particles approach they become influenced by various radiation belts that surround the Earth resulting in a concentration of activity at the Earth's Magnetic Poles (Auroral Zones). The result is an Aurora which often can be seen visually as a display of light and appropriately known in the Northern Hemisphere as the 'Northern Lights'. However the activity is not only seen as visual effects but it also produces ionospheric and magnetic storms within the D, E and F layers, producing a disruption of radio communications.

The Aurora produces a reflecting sheet, which lies in a more vertical plane and it is possible to obtain reflection off this sheet at VHF. As the Auroral sheet lies to the North, it follows that the transmitted signal will be received from a Northerly direction, rather than the true direction of the transmitter, which may be in another direction. It would appear easier to obtain a signal reflection at 90° from the sheet, however signal reflection at extremely narrow angles is possible.

There is a tendency for a twenty-seven day re-occurrence from a very large flare due to the rotation of the Sun. A flare situated towards the centre of the Sun will produce considerably more Auroral activity than a flare located on the outer limbs of the Sun. The Equinoxes are the most favoured time for Auroral activity, when either the Sun's North or South Pole tilts towards the Earth, occurring during April and October.

As a general rule aerials should be pointed towards the North varying between North-East and North-

West. Frequencies mainly affected are in Bands 1 and 2, although signals have at times been noted up to 200 MHz. On rare occasions, signals have been received across the North Atlantic. Vision signals tend to be poorly propagated via Auroral reflection, generally suffering with severe smearing and distortion. Characteristics of this propagation mode are hum bars on vision accompanied with a rumbling noise on sound. Auroral activity tends to produce two phases of propagation at VHF, an afternoon and a later evening phase have been noted, either phase may be the stronger.

Lightning Scatter

Experience has shown that signal reflection may be obtained from the effects of lightning flashes. It would appear that intense localised ionisation occurs in the air around the lightning stroke, this ionisation being of sufficient density to support signal reflection at frequencies through VHF and to the lower UHF spectrum over distances reaching to 500 miles. Such signals are of short duration — resembling meteor scatter — and the lightning flash itself needs to be on or near the transmitter/receiver path. A storm tracking across the signal path at 90° to the midpoint of the path would provide optimum conditions for such signal reflection. Sheet lightning can undoubtedly provide more positive results than fork lightning. A number of enthusiasts have exploited this medium and confirmed signal reception from transmitters operating at Band 1, 3 and UHF at distances up to 500 miles.

Aircraft Scatter

With the rapid increasing number of enthusiasts in the long distance television field so has been noted the reports of signal reception in the VHF/UHF bands of transmission at distances up to 400 miles, the signals having the characteristic of a typical Meteor Scatter type namely short bursts of a few seconds but of course at too short a distance for MS. It was eventually established that the signals were reflections from high flying aircraft. A number of enthusiasts have erected aerials capable of movement in both bearing and elevation and recorded some success with VHF and UHF signal reflection from high flying aircraft on established flight paths. Such an activity requires a great deal of patience and dedication since the transmissions that are normally received by such a reflective mode are available relatively easily during a slight Tropospheric lift by conventional receiving methods.

Field Aligned Irregularities (FAI)

Towards the end of the 1970s and with increasing Sunspot activity, instances were recorded of signal reception at both VHF and UHF but at frequencies that would not be supported by F2/TE propagation. Research has established that high density bubbles of an elongated shape are aligned within the Earth's magnetic field (i.e. on a North/South path predominently) and giving rise to signal reception within an area ± 2000 miles of the Equator, similar to the evening TE phenomena. The intensity of the 'bubbles' are such that radio amateur signals at 432 MHz have been received at distances of 4000 miles. FAI has a characteristic weak and fluttery signal and occurs during the evening period. FAI is associated with high Sunspot activity and is most likely to be received in the Equinoxes (March—May and September—November).

RECEIVER REQUIREMENTS

A television receiver intended for long distance reception has requirements somewhat more demanding than that of a receiver intended for 'normal' domestic use. Unlike the domestic receiver the long distance equivalent has to work with extremes of signal strength, from a few microvolts (μV) of a deep fringe or fading Tropospheric signal, to the extremely high and fluctuating strength encountered with Sporadic E signals. Receiver gain therefore has to be of a high order whilst maintaining complete stability, freedom from overload and associated effects. At times reception may be sought on an adjacent channel to that of a high powered local transmitter, which calls for a high degree of IF selectivity and adjacent channel rejection. The AGC (Automatic Gain Control) within the IF strip and tuner should be capable of some adjustment for certain expected types of signal, whilst retaining sufficient versatility to cope with the extremes of signal strength and for short bursts of MS (Meteor Shower/Scatter). The accuracy of tuning adjustment/channel setting is of paramount importance to ensure that anticipated weak or short duration signals (e.g. Plane scatter, MS etc.) are received at optimum strength.

The IF strip itself amplifies the signal from the tuner up to the order of one volt, at the video detector, prior to feeding the signal to the video amplifier(s) and it is desirable that this is accomplished with the minimum of noise possible. The wide versus narrow video IF bandwidth question will be discussed later with its relationship to the noise problem but sufficient to say at this stage that a wide IF bandwidth — necessary for both sound and video signals — will tend to have a lower gain and higher noise than that of a narrower IF bandwidth for video only. In most British receivers only one high gain video amplifier stage is used — in the case of valves — but it is common Continental practice to have two stages of video amplification, the synchronisation information being taken off after the first stage. With solid state receivers the output from the video detector(s) is normally passed through a video driver stage prior to the video amplifier. Synchronisation information passes to the Synchronising Separator stage, where the line and field synchronisation pulses are separated and directed to the appropriate timebase stages. The type and ability of the synchronising separator stage will vary between receivers, in some designs various amplification and clipping stages may be incorporated. Here, as with other stages, extremely weak signals will be encountered and a first class performance is required for reception of marginal signals. Flywheel Synchronisation, a circuit that allows for improved locking within the line timebase must be regarded as an essential. The requirements for sound reception are somewhat less demanding, apart from high gain and a low noise figure.

In general terms receivers encountered will use solid state technology though at an enthusiast level valve receivers may still be used — particularly the vintage dual standard 405/625 line UK standard — exploiting the wide/narrow IF strip selectivity potential. For completeness this revised volume will retain earlier notes relating to the use of valves in the various circuits applicable to TV-DXing work.

TUNERS

With the growth of the UHF network throughout the United Kingdom so has seen the demise of the VHF tuner being fitted in current production receivers since the 625 line System I transmission is at UHF only. System I is however used in the Irish Republic at both VHF and UHF and receivers destined for this market will have provision for coverage of both frequency spectrums. Before manufacture of the System A receiver ceased, the general practice had been to use both transistor and valve tuners and when selecting a receiver for use in long distance reception the valve VHF tuner is to be preferred. The improvement in using transistors over valves at VHF is far less marked than at UHF and there are certain advantages with the use of valves. The bi-polar transistor tends to be rather susceptible to overload and on frequencies closely adjacent to high powered transmissions interference and cross modulation effects may be experienced. The transistor being a low impedance device and with a resulting wider bandwidth property will tend to spread a strong signal over adjacent frequencies, whereas a valve circuit has a more linear response and is far less prone to such problems.

Signals experienced with Tropospheric reception are often of the order of a few μV when arriving at the receiver input and a very low noise amplification is required if we are to avoid the signal being lost in Mixer and IF strip noise.

The VHF tuner may be of several types. The type often encountered is the Turret Tuner. This contains coil biscuits for each channel required. In the Americas where only System M signals are likely to

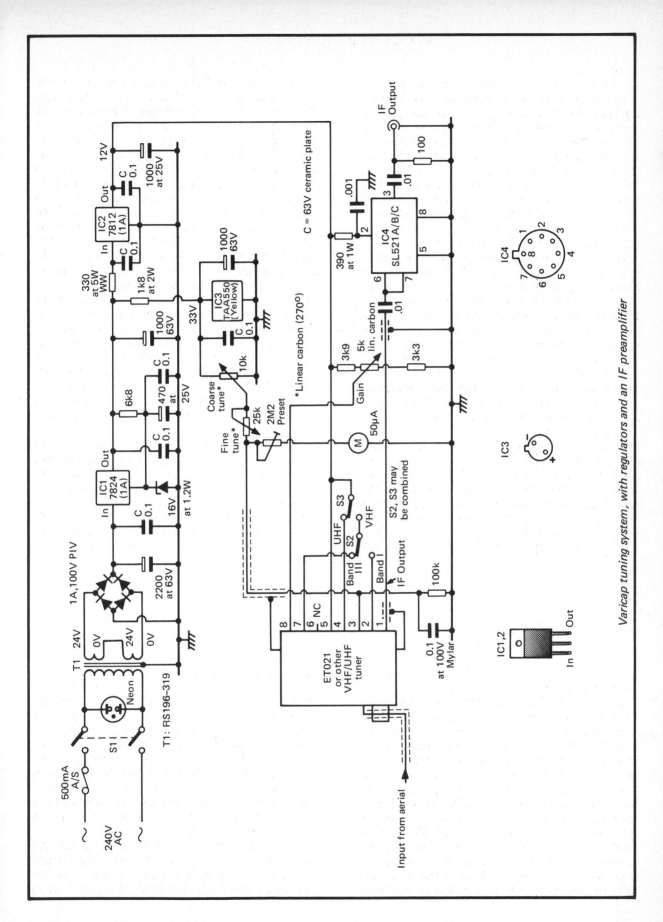

Varicap tuning system, with regulators and an IF preamplifier

19

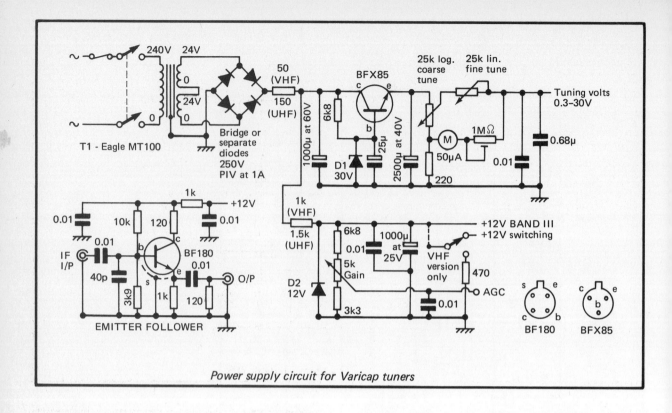

Power supply circuit for Varicap tuners

be experienced, the tuner can be loaded with coils for channels A2 — A13 inclusive and there are no further problems. In Europe however, with the multiplicity of transmission standards and channel allocations, a considerable number of coils will be required to cover all the channels liable to be received.

The transistor UHF tuner has undoubtedly ousted the valve UHF tuner on grounds of improved gain and noise figures. In the European area the UHF tuner will always be found with a tuned RF amplifier, although it should be noted that some manufacturers use only three gang tuning — the input to the RF amplifier being untuned (Aperiodic Input). Where possible the four gang tuning types should be used for the improved selectivity which will be useful on channels adjacent to high powered local transmitters.

Unfortunately, in the Americas, RF amplification stages are rarely fitted to UHF tuners, the tuned aerial input being coupled directly into the Mixer stage.

The Varicap tuner — a device which uses variable capacity diodes instead of the more conventional means of tuning — is in use for both VHF and UHF applications. The selectivity and adjacent channel rejection problems are similar to the conventional transistor tuner, some Varicap UHF tuners are fitted with two tuned RF stages. The German company Telefunken have placed on the market for receiver manufacturers VHF/UHF tuners with MOSFETS fitted in the RF and mixer stages of the VHF section, for use in areas subject to adjacent channel selectivity problems. Typical figures quoted for an interfering signal two channels away from the desired signal and to give a 1% cross modulation on the desired signal are 100 mV as compared to a conventional varicap bipolar tuner with 25 mV (Band 3 channels).

At the time of writing MOSFET tuners are available on the surplus market for both VHF/UHF though the reader is advised to check stock listings from surplus dealers for updated availability of suitable equipment.

The Varicap does however allow a freedom of operation not previously experienced on the conventional VHF tuner. Since it is possible to 'sweep' through all frequencies in Bands 1 and 3, the various channels currently operating in the European area may be received easily, far more so than aligning many individual turret tuner biscuit coils. Varicap tuners for both VHF and UHF are commonly available from component suppliers and an efficient circuit providing power, variable gain, band switching (in the case of the VHF version), coarse and fine tuning is shown. It is possible to modify a conventional VHF tuner, mounted as standard in a receiver, to act as an IF preamplifier. By injecting the IF output of the Varicap tuner unit into the modified VHF tuner a very high gain receiving installation may be obtained.

There is available a transistor unit known as an 'Upconverter' which can facilitate receiving VHF signals on a 'UHF only' receiver. This unit is basically a VHF to UHF converter and converts the whole 40 — 250 MHz spectrum to an equivalent range at UHF thus enabling a standard UHF tuner to tune over the

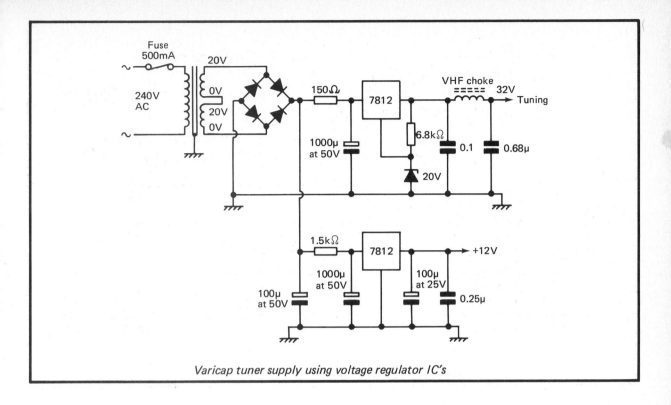

Varicap tuner supply using voltage regulator IC's

complete frequency band at VHF as above. The unit was originally intended for use with communal aerial systems where losses at UHF would be prohibitive. The UHF channels are converted at the head amplifiers to VHF and distributed throughout the system, reconversion back to UHF is then carried out on each individual subscriber's receiver via the upconverter.

Since these units are wide band in operation they provide an extremely effective means of covering all channels at VHF including those channels that lie outside the range of most VHF tuners namely chs. R3, 4, 5 and ch.IC.

Several manufacturers now produce these converter units which incorporate a wideband RF amplifier input stage covering the full input designed bandwidth of 40 — 250 MHz and suitable for use on low level signals.

Great care should be taken to avoid overloading the unit with excessive signal input since successive stages in the receiving chain will tend to exaggerate the condition.

For operational ease the use of push button tuners should be avoided. The turret tuner does allow each channel to be switched to with ease and indeed the

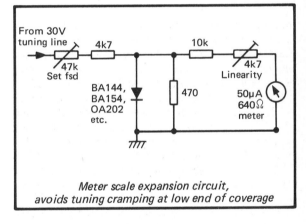

Meter scale expansion circuit,
avoids tuning cramping at low end of coverage

slow motion mechanical UHF tuner is to be preferred. With the advent of the Varicap tuner direct channel reading may be taken off of a suitable meter movement, in such cases it is advisable to maintain a table of meter/channel settings. In passing it should be noted that many European manufactured tuners have extended VHF coverage from Band 1 through to Band 2 at 100 MHz enabling easy coverage of Band 2 (TV).

The IF strip (Intermediate Frequency Amplifiers) accept the IF output from the VHF (or UHF) tuner and amplifies the required signal to approximately one volt at the detector prior to feeding the video amplifier(s) It is within this section that the main IF response is determined; the VHF tuner consisting of effectively wide band circuits.

In passing, some earlier UK dual standard TV receivers utilised the VHF tuner in whole or part to act as an IF preamplifier stage when operating at UHF. If a valve receiver is to be used then 3 vision IF stages are ideal and if possible 4 stages in the case of a solid state receiver fitted with discrete devices – though with present day IC technology distributed in the mass produced TV receiver an additional IF gain/shaping stage could possibly be fitted prior to the main IF strip input – see later. This number of stages if necessary to obtain the required gain/bandwidth performance; bearing in mind the transmitted signal information may have a bandwidth of up to 8 MHz.

Although weak signals produce problems undoubtedly an equal problem is interference from high powered transmitters, thus effectively limiting the use of high gain aerial amplifiers due to various forms of adjacent and co-channel interference. One way of surmounting such a problem is to include various filters and traps within the IF strip, to remove the offending interference from adjacent channels and frequencies. Generally most receivers will have insufficient filtering and additional traps can be added to improve the adjacent channel rejection. If one

particular transmitter causes a problem an aerial notch filter can be fitted, but it should be borne in mind that during periods of enhanced reception, strong signals are likely to appear on otherwise unoccupied channels – producing further problems. Consequently the IF strip should incorporate all the filtering and traps necessary to give good adjacent rejection either side of any channel in use.

It had become a practice within the United Kingdom to make use of suitably modified System A receivers, with their narrower bandwidth video IF strip (3 MHz). Such a narrow IF bandwidth results in an increased gain with a considerably lower noise figure, allowing reception of extremely weak signals which on a System B receiver (5 MHz video bandwidth) would be marred by noise. This does tend to show a lack of HF detail if the signal becomes extremely strong but the loss is well worthwhile with marginal signals. An additional advantage is that with the multiplicity of transmission standards within Europe and closely adjacent channel allocations, a narrow IF bandwidth receiver is able to tune to each signal, whereas with a System B receiver, adjacent channels tend to float over each other (an example being ch.E2/1). The advantage of a narrow IF bandwidth is only too obvious during a prolonged Sporadic E opening! Where possible the provision of adding wide/narrow bandwidth switching within the IF strip should be investigated. With a narrow video IF bandwidth the sound channel of System B and other similar standards using Intercarrier sound will of course be lost. The demise of 405 line

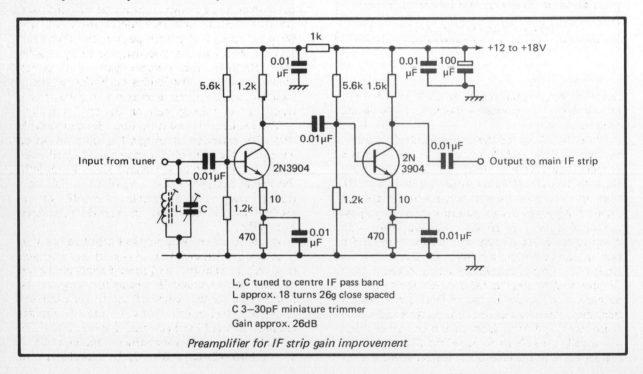

L, C tuned to centre IF pass band
L approx. 18 turns 26g close spaced
C 3–30pF miniature trimmer
Gain approx. 26dB

Preamplifier for IF strip gain improvement

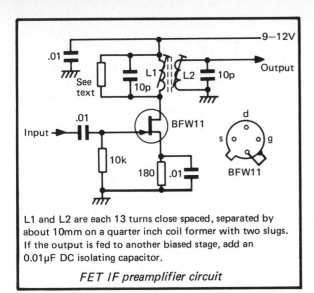

L1 and L2 are each 13 turns close spaced, separated by about 10mm on a quarter inch coil former with two slugs. If the output is fed to another biased stage, add an 0.01µF DC isolating capacitor.

FET IF preamplifier circuit

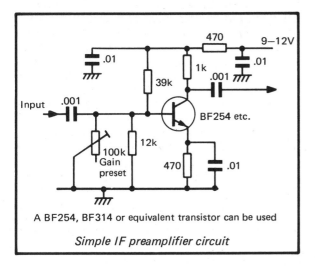

A BF254, BF314 or equivalent transistor can be used

Simple IF preamplifier circuit

receivers means that other methods of achieving narrow vision IF bandwidths should be explored and exploited.

With the advent of the single standard System I receiver into the United Kingdom so have IF strips become somewhat less versatile, at least with a view for long distance television usage. Printed circuit IF coils have come into common use with little or no means of adjustment, and the fitting of multi-purpose integrated circuits in IF strips had dispensed with many of the tuned circuits once associated with this part of the television receiver. IF shaping in this latter type of receiver is usually accomplished with an IF preamplifier stage fitted between the tuner's IF output and the input to the main IF strip. Such a stage may comprise one or two transistors and several tuned circuits, if these latter circuits are variable then it is usually possible to 're-shape' the IF response to a sharper curve in the interests of greater selectivity. It

may be advisable to fit a second IF preamplifier stage and adjust the latter rather than disturb the receiver's main response, then either the first stage (wide selectivity) or second stage (narrow selectivity) may be switched into circuit. Such a preamplifier stage may be fitted into a receiver having printed circuit IF coils, thus improving both the IF selectivity and overall gain figures. With the increasing use of Surface Acoustic Wave Filters (SAWF) in modern IF strips, adjustment of the response curve will be extremely difficult and in such receivers it may be possible to construct an IF preamplifier stage and obtain the required selectivity performance. A relatively simple 2 stage IF preamplifier is shown that gives a useful gain of approximately 26 dB. Being a wideband circuit the bandpass characteristic is determined by the tuned circuit L and C at the circuit input. A further tuned circuit can be added at the output prior to connection to the main receiver's IF strip.

In modern receivers IF circuitry may be contained in one or more discrete modules and in certain of the Philips range these are designated as an IF selectivity unit and an IF gain board. The former contains several tuneable coils and a single transistor stage whereas the latter features the bulk of the IF gain and with minimal coil adjustment. Since the IF selectivity unit adjusts the overall shape of the IF bandpass it follows that the fittings of this module into any receiver of similar IF will enable modification of the IF bandpass by careful adjustment of the module's coils. It is possible to fit a module of this type in series with the IF input feed from the receiver's tuner(s) to the main IF strip and 'peak' up the module to provide a restricted bandpass and hence improved selectivity. In certain circumstances two such modules have been inserted in series to give sharp selectivity. It is then possible to either insert into circuit for narrow selectivity or to by-pass for wide selectivity with a simple slide switch or pin diode switching. The Philips G8/U800 selectivity module is available from television spares dealers and from time to time appears on the surplus market.

The reduced IF bandwidth does give considerable help with reception of marginal satellite originated TV signals, the trade-off for an improved signal/noise figure against that of a reduced video bandwidth. Experience has shown that a signal not visible on a receiver using an IF bandwidth of 5 MHz, can be resolved using a receiver with its bandwidth restricted to 2.5 MHz.

In the Americas with only one standard likely to be received – that of System M – particular attention need only be paid to the adjacent channel protection figures. Often a simple IF preamplifier stage can be fitted tuned to the centre of the IF passband and using only two notch filters – that of adjacent channel video (LF) and adjacent channel audio (HF).

With the three main sound/vision spacings of 5.5, 6, 6.5 MHz (Systems B/G, I, D respectively), so

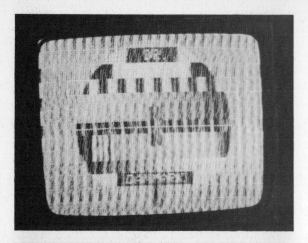

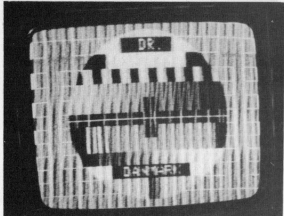

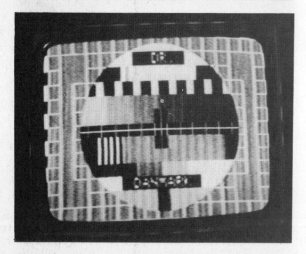

The effects of progressively reducing IF bandwidth in the presence of high level adjacent channel (System B) interference. C1 = 6 MHz; C2 = 3MHz; C3 = 2 MHz

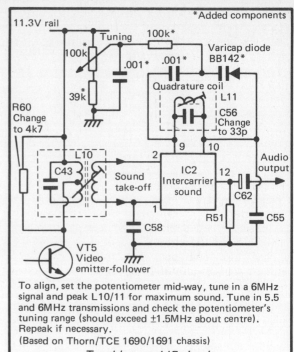

To align, set the potentiometer mid-way, tune in a 6MHz signal and peak L10/11 for maximum sound. Tune in 5.5 and 6MHz transmissions and check the potentiometer's tuning range (should exceed ±1.5MHz about centre). Repeak if necessary.
(Based on Thorn/TCE 1690/1691 chassis)

Tunable sound IF circuit

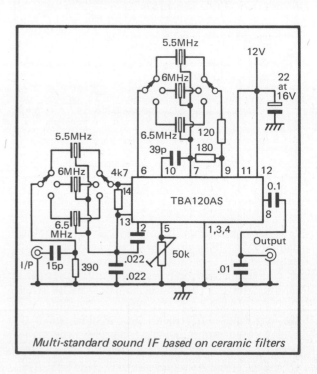

Multi-standard sound IF based on ceramic filters

efficient coverage of the matching sound signals — when in a wide IF bandpass mode and using a single standard receiver — is extremely difficult. Several experienced enthusiasts have successfully modified their receivers (that use an IC type sound IF) by switched varicap diode tuning of the sound take-off

and IC detector coils. Since only two tuned circuits are involved, 3 position preset switching can be incorporated relatively easily although correct setting up may prove difficult without relevant test equipment.

The use of ceramic filters for 5.5, 6, 6.5 MHz (again available from surplus houses) eases construction of multi-standard sound sections — a 6.5 MHz filter can often be found in the UK if lists and advertisements are closely scrutinized. Reduced vision IF bandwidth operation will obviously lead to a loss of intercarrier sound. If an FM radio covering 30–50 MHz (USA 'Low Band PMR') can be found it may be used as a tunable IF to cover the various sound carrier offsets by tapping from the TV tuner IF output via a single stage splitter amplifier (e.g. BFY90 + star network).

Selective IF Amplifier Stage

A narrow bandpass video IF amplifier stage is shown, based on commonly available Toko coils. This circuit is best inserted as the first active stage after the tuner IF output and can of course be switched into and out of circuit as reception dictates. A bandwidth of 2 MHz should be obtained when 'peaked'. Alignment is simple, tune to a weak but steady non-fading signal, insert this amplifier stage into circuit and peak each transformer from the output through to the input for optimum signal/minimal noise. Provided normal VHF construction techniques are applied, i.e. short lead lengths, the amplifier will work efficiently and with no instability.

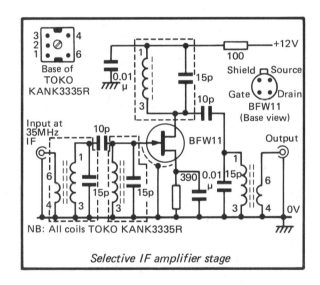

Selective IF amplifier stage

Outboard Conversion Systems for TV-DXing

With the demise of the UK VHF TV receiver, enthusiasts have generally followed the simple 'upconverter' approach for VHF coverage (conversion of wideband VHF to an equivalent spectrum bandwidth at UHF for tuning with a standard UHF tuner) or merely invested in a multi-band/multi-standard TV receiver for TV-DXing. Though there are shortcomings in the above types of equipment for the serious TV-DXer, there is an obvious reluctance to modify an expensive newly purchased receiver to improve its weak signal/DX performance.

The upconverter system can however be exploited

to give a comprehensive DX facility whilst retaining the receiver itself in a completely unmodified state acting as an RF VDU with all signal processing accomplished before the receiver aerial socket.

The writer has operated over several years an IF processor system which provides switched IF selectivity bandwidths between 6 down to 2 MHz (reducing vision bandwidths still further enters a problem of image detail resolution — smearing, etc.), in a relatively simple and basic outboard construction. Some constructional ability is necessary to make a processor system, though the building block approach is fairly simple and can be adopted to suit a given situation/requirement and skill.

In the basic IF processor system an outboard VHF/UHF tuner is used, completely independent from the main TV. The IF output is connected to the VHF input of an upconverter, the output of the upconverter is in turn connected to the main TV aerial socket, the TV itself being tuned to match the upconverted IF signal, usually at approximately ch.30 with the typical commercial upconverter. Thus full VHF/UHF tuning coverage is obtained by adjustment of the outboard tuner, the main TV tuning once set to the upconverted IF and the UHF output frequency being left untouched.

Filtering of the IF signal to restrict the passband width and thus achieve variable IF selectivity is fitted at the IF output of the outboard tuner prior to the upconverter input. Processing at this point allows full retention of the received signal characteristics (i.e. vestigial sideband, sound/vision spacing, etc.). A full IF strip/video demodulation circuit — constructed perhaps from surplus equipment — could of course be used with video remodulation to UHF via a standard video modulator. Demodulation to baseband video could provide both + and — going video senses with remodulation back to a standard System I vision format, though sound provision to System I would require a special dual input modulator (use of a vision modulator will result in a double sideband vision signal). The standard video modulator can upconvert an IF signal input to UHF though the drive level needs to be relatively high to gain an adequate UHF conversion output.

The IF upconverter approach is therefore the preferred technique with filtering and frequency conversion at low level.

A basic filtering circuit is shown giving a wide/narrow IF bandpass — obviously in 'narrow' at approximately 3 MHz sound would be lost. Alignment is simple; the collector IF transformer is 'peaked' in the 'wide' IF bandpass setting to give optimum signal transference within the required IF frequency band, the heavy damping producing a very shallow peak. Switching to 'narrow' inserts the 2 tuned circuits via BA182 diodes. These 2 circuits are peaked on a weak signal — the improvement in selectivity and signal/noise is dramatic. The collector transformer is left untouched in the

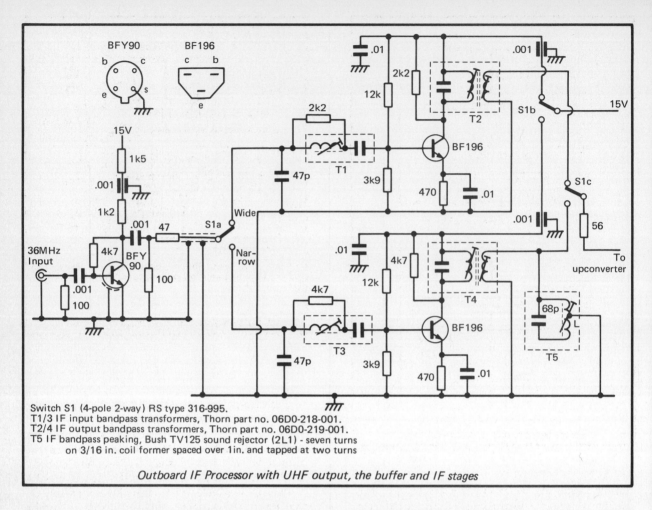

BFY90

BF196

Switch S1 (4-pole 2-way) RS type 316-995.
T1/3 IF input bandpass transformers, Thorn part no. 06D0-218-001.
T2/4 IF output bandpass transformers, Thorn part no. 06D0-219-001.
T5 IF bandpass peaking, Bush TV125 sound rejector (2L1) - seven turns
    on 3/16 in. coil former spaced over 1 in. and tapped at two turns

Outboard IF Processor with UHF output, the buffer and IF stages

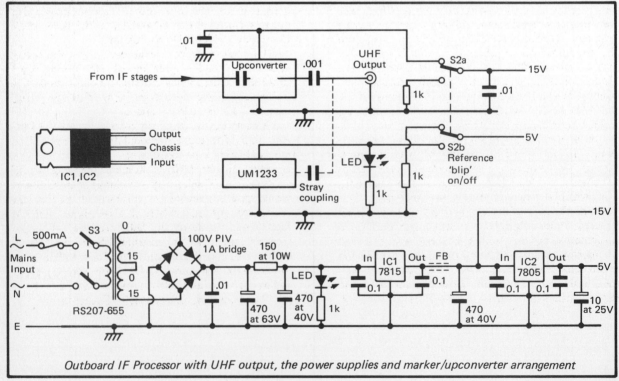

Outboard IF Processor with UHF output, the power supplies and marker/upconverter arrangement

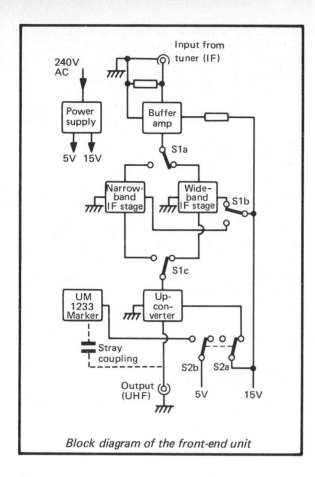

Block diagram of the front-end unit

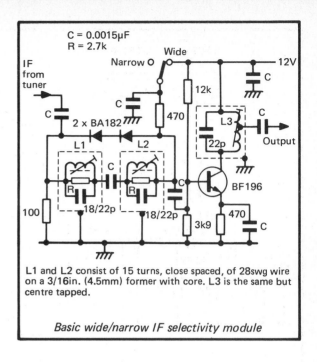

C = 0.0015µF
R = 2.7k

L1 and L2 consist of 15 turns, close spaced, of 28swg wire on a 3/16in. (4.5mm) former with core. L3 is the same but centre tapped.

Basic wide/narrow IF selectivity module

'narrow' alignment operation. In general no modification is necessary with the upconverter unless high pass filtering is fitted at its input circuit (which may well attenuate signals below 40 MHz); should filtering be present then it is removed to avoid attenuation of the IF signal input. The 'Marker' UHF modulator give a reference 'blip' when 5 V is applied. The Modulator is peaked to the output processor frequency, this enables easy and correct tuning of the main TV receiver (UHF) to match with the processor output for optimum signal transference.

An alternative approach to the above constructional project is with the use of manufacturers' surplus TV components and modules — the Philips G8 chassis for example features a vision IF selectivity 'can' which is fitted to the main chassis pcb. This contains the various IF shaping tuned circuits and can be used in its original or 'peaked' alignment (or a combination of both with a 'peaked' being switched for narrow bandpass) condition. Companion to the vision selectivity 'can' is a vision gain 'can' that contains both IF main gain and video demodulation, the output sufficient to drive a video UHF modulator.

A second vision gain 'can' could be modified for + going video and fitted in switched parallel to offer System L video facility. The G8/U800 modules are much sought after by DX enthusiasts and appear from time to time in the 'new' surplus market.

With the growth of the IC IF strip so a self-contained IF selectivity/IF strip/video demodulator can be found in very compact form. Certain dedicated TV ICs have both + and − going video outputs (such as the TDA4420) sufficient to drive the standard video/UHF modulator.

The above gives examples of alternative approaches to the problem of RF tuning/signal processing and avoiding extensive modification to a TV receiver, the advantage being that the main receiver is left completely intact.

Using the above 'building block' approach, a vari-cap tuned FM sound demodulator covering 5.5 to 6.5 MHz could be considered, though if a radio covering 30–40 MHz is available tapping at IF (prior to any IF selectivity switching) as an RF input would give comprehensive coverage of all incident sound spacings, particularly if a switchable AM/FM facility is available on the radio receiver. A simple receiver could even be constructed based on 'Denco' coils. The USA 'Low Band' for PMR, police communications etc. uses 30–50 MHz and imported radios become available at times with this band fitted and are ideal for a tuneable IF receiver.

The IF strip terminates in the video detector which rectifies the incoming IF signal prior to the video amplifier(s). Although circuitry here is conventional, again in Europe with reception of either positive or negative going video, switching has to be incorporated. Many European television receivers incorporate such switching together with the necessary IF adjustments for both video and sound (and timebases where necessary). Consequently little problem should be experienced with receiving either video standard on such receivers. However for the single standard receiver, a second video detector diode should be fitted — with low loss switching and wiring — enabling either standard to be resolved. Generally some adjustment to video amplifier bias should be made when switching can be incorporated upon the same switching assembly as the detector(s). Assuming a positive going video receiver is being modified to switch to negative video, a reduction in cathode bias on the video amplifier is all that is usually required. Comparison should be made with circuits of commercial receivers that incorporate video switching, from which source similar circuit information can be extracted.

Four typical video detector circuits are illustrated that give provision for positive or negative video signals to be selected. The valve circuit may be found in the more elderly receivers and generally was superseded by the semiconductor circuit shown in figure (b). These circuits can be incorporated in a single standard receiver to provide switching between 2 video standards but extreme care must be taken to minimise connecting lead lengths in the interests of gain and stability. In many solid state receivers an emitter follower stage follows the video detector and this can be modified relatively easily to provide positive and negative switching (+ video at collector, − video at emitter). A small switch may be used to select either video sense and since the video is at low impedance, connecting leads may be permitted to be slightly longer than when modifications are made directly onto the detector. Figure (c) gives a typical video phase splitter which can be fitted into a single standard IF strip or in the case of a receiver already fitted with an emitter follower between video detector/video amplifier this can be modified to values similar to figure (c). An AGC feed may be found in certain receivers from the emitter of the

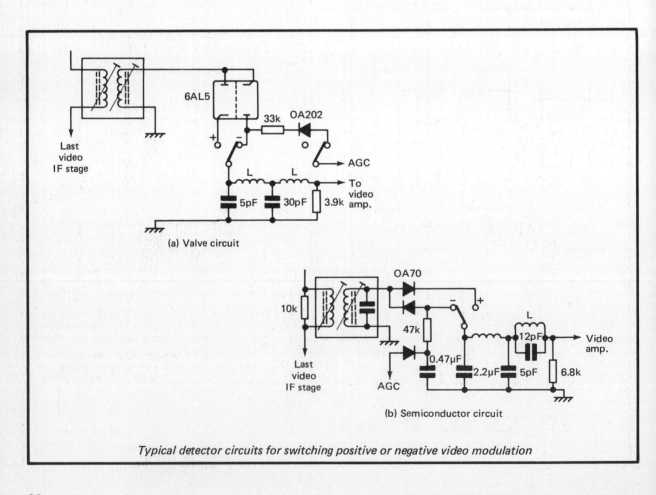

Typical detector circuits for switching positive or negative video modulation

video emitter follower stage. This should be left as the operation of the AGC circuits will be unaltered by the video phase splitting modifications. Only the very experienced should attempt modifications of a receiver using ICs incorporating video detection.

Figure (d) illustrates a modern detector circuit

using discrete components in which a phase splitter could be fitted, showing the final IF stage, detector, video driver. The AGC feed is taken from the AGC amplifier stage as + going for an increasing gain reduction, line pulses being fed via W3 from the line output stage to obtain a control voltage in proportion to sync information at the base of VT6. A sophisticated +/− switching video amplifier offers an alternative means for System L display which is detailed at the end of this section.

From the video amplifier(s), one output is taken as drive to the cathode ray tube and another to the Synchronising Separator. This stage extracts the various line and field pulses necessary to synchronise the appropriate timebases. Various types of synchronising separators will be found, one particularly efficient version is the noise gated type which is suitable for deep fringe work. Various clipping and amplification stages may be found indicating its suitability for weak signal work. Of the utmost importance is a receiver incorporating Flywheel Synchronisation which is essential for any long

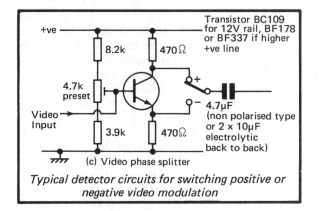

Typical detector circuits for switching positive or negative video modulation

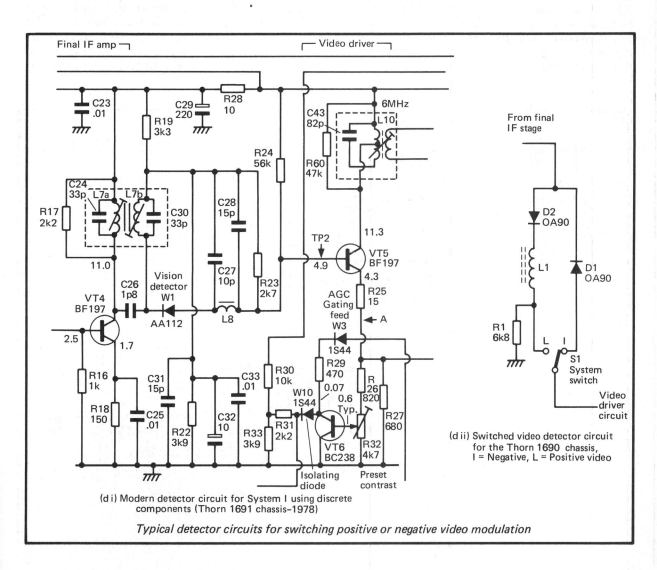

(d i) Modern detector circuit for System I using discrete components (Thorn 1691 chassis–1978)

(d ii) Switched video detector circuit for the Thorn 1690 chassis, I = Negative, L = Positive video

Typical detector circuits for switching positive or negative video modulation

distance television work. The synchronisation of the timebases must be accurate and correct, as certain signals such as Meteor Shower (MS) produce very short bursts of signal which necessitates immediate locking if the signal is to be identified. Often it is possible to improve the filtering and performance of the synchronisation separator stage for such weak signal work. One new system coming into use which improves field sync locking makes use of a count down system. Basically line sync pulses are divided down developing a field sync signal to give correct field lock immediately on signal reception. This system obviates the need for a field hold and field oscillator stage and early reports indicate its suitability for extremely weak signal work. Generally the sync separator stage has little scope for modification and apart from experimenting with increased filtering and increased values of sync coupling components the section should be left unaltered.

Often derived from the sync separator stage is a negative going voltage which after filtering is applied as IF amplifier bias (in the case of valves), reducing the gain on strong signals and vice versa. Such a system is known as Mean Level AGC (Automatic Gain Control); the voltage being dependent upon the average brightness of the video signal. Other systems derive AGC voltage from the line output stage known as Line Gated AGC and Sync Pulse – cancelled AGC. Solid state receivers differ somewhat with AGC circuitry and often incorporate an AGC amplifier stage to derive controlled stages, reference signal levels again may be sampled on sync pulse intervals or from the video stages.

The AGC voltage to the RF amplifier is usually delayed in an endeavour to maintain best signal/ noise figure possible, in certain single standard System A receivers of the 1960s an adjustable delay could be selected for optimum picture quality. Often the RF amplifier within the VHF tuner has provision to be switched to either the delayed AGC or to chassis, the latter position enabling an improved signal/noise performance. The time constant of the AGC line is normally fixed but with an advanced receiver a switched time constant may prove invaluable, especially with Meteor Shower (MS) signals, which by their nature are extremely short in duration and with a wide range of signal strengths. One disadvantage with gated AGC systems occurs when a signal suffers from a severe ghosting or multiple images. A negative ghost can cancel the synchronisation thus reducing the efficiency of the AGC system.

The timebases themselves are conventional but it is necessary for them to remain stable for long periods Again in Europe there are several line standards which need to be catered for. Fortunately information for such adjustments on a System A receiver that may be required can be obtained easily by scrutinising multiple standard television receiver circuits and generally any modifications can be accomplished quite easily. It is a general practice to

Teletext information is now widely transmitted in Europe as this example from WDR-1, West Germany shows. Teletext can be resolved on a TV-DXing basis if the signal received suffers minimal fading

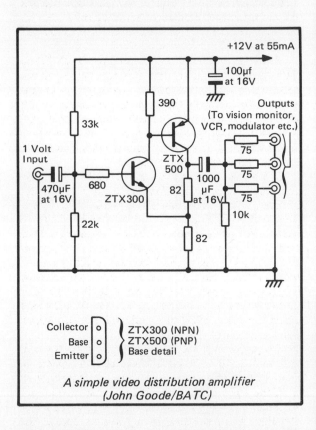

A simple video distribution amplifier (John Goode/BATC)

feed the field oscillator from the boost HT line in the interests of stability. There may be a tendency with some receivers on fast fading signals for the line oscillator to fall out of synchronisation for short periods during such deep fades. At such times the boost HT may alter somewhat, causing the field oscillator to alter in frequency and producing a roll. It may prove useful to connect the field oscillator, suitably decoupled, to the receiver main HT line.

Power supplies are conventional but it should be

borne in mind that within the United Kingdom it is common practice to find live chassis technique (AD/DC). Consequently great care must be taken whilst operating or adjusting receivers with protective covers removed. Death is so permanent!

A simple vision distribution amplifier circuit is featured that accepts baseband composite video input to 1 volt and provides up to 5 outputs into 75 ohms for feeding a monitor(s), VCR and other sources One feed can be used to provide an RF (UHF) signal output via a standard modulator for connection to a standard domestic TV.

SWITCHABLE +/− VIDEO AMPLIFIER
(Designed by D. Lauder)

This circuit allows either French System 'L' positive modulation vision signals or normal negative modulation signals to be received on a TV which is designed for negative modulation only (such as any single standard British TV). This circuit does not alter the colour signal so colour reception requires a TV with SECAM capability and neither does it allow the System 'L' AM sound to be received.

Receiving System 'L' used to be easy for TV-DXers with converted 405/625 line TVs but is not so simple for modern single standard TVs. Switching round the vision detector diode (if there is one) is not usually easy as it can lead to IF instability or incorrect AGC operation. With integrated circuit vision detectors there is usually no simple modification unless the IC has a second inverted video output.

The best solution for most modern TVs is to leave the vision detector as it is and to fit a switchable inverting/non-inverting amplifier in the video path. The circuit described is DC coupled throughout and is suitable for a wide range of TVs. Several have been built and it is a tried and tested design. The transistors used are cheap general purpose silicon types and with no bulky electrolytic capacitors. The selection of inverting or non-inverting mode is *DC Controlled* so the wiring to the mode switch can be long as it carries no video, allowing the video input and output connections to be kept short.

The amplifier has almost unity gain in both modes and its −3 dB bandwidth is typically 10 MHz. It should be fitted into the video path so that it inverts both the video to the tube *and* the video to the sync separator. The input must be fed from a point where the video has a standing DC voltage on it such that the video waveform does not go below +1 volt and does not go higher than 60% of the supply voltage (+7.2 V with a 12 V supply). The input impedance is about 50 kΩ at low frequencies and the input must be driven from a point which can supply approximately 0.1 mA of base bias current for TR1.

There are two versions of this circuit. The normal one is the simpler unbuffered version which has an output impedance of 470 Ω and a current consumption of typically 25 mA (with +12 V supply and +5 V on the input). This is suitable for driving the base of a following transistor stage and/or a load of 10 kΩ or more. Where it is necessary to drive a lower impedance (approx. 50 Ω) and higher current consumption (typically 40 mA under the above conditions). It is not suitable for driving 1 V p-p video into a 50 Ω or 75 Ω terminated load however.

The supply voltage should be 9–18 volts. If it is too low compared to the peak positive video input voltage, TR3 or TR4 will saturate causing white areas of the picture to spread to the right. TR1 and TR2 are NPN such as BC237 or 2N3904. TR3, TR4, and TR5 (if required) are PNP such as BC307, 2N3906. Other general purpose silicon transistors can be used provided they are not excessively high frequency types and provided the lead out sequence is E-B-C or C-B-E (check carefully!). Capacitors should be 0.1 μF disc ceramic. Resistors should be ± 5% or better, 1/8 watt rating. If experimenting with different resistor values, the following relations should be preserved: R6 = R7 = exactly 1.5 times R5. R1 = R2 = R3 = R4 = 2 to 3 times R5.

For the normal unbuffered version, R8, R9 and TR5 are *not* fitted but Link 'A' and D3 *are* fitted. For the buffered version, R8, R9 and TR5 *are* fitted, Link 'A' is *not* fitted and D3 is replaced by a short circuit.

Testing
It is worth testing the circuit before fitting it to the TV set. All voltages are measured relative to GROUND pin unless otherwise stated. Connect a battery such as PP7, PP9 or a DC power supply of 9–18 volts with −ve to the GROUND pin and +ve to V+ pin. A 250 mA fuse or current limited power supply is recommended. With the INPUT and MODE pins not connected the voltage on the OUTPUT pin should be 0 V (+0.7 V for the buffered version). Temporarily connect 10 kΩ resistor between the INPUT pin and GROUND and 15 kΩ between INPUT pin and V+. The voltages on the INPUT and OUTPUT pins should be approximately 40% of the supply voltage. A voltmeter connected between the INPUT and OUTPUT pins should register ±0.1 volt or less. Now connect the MODE pin to +V. With VR1 wiper at the ground end

31

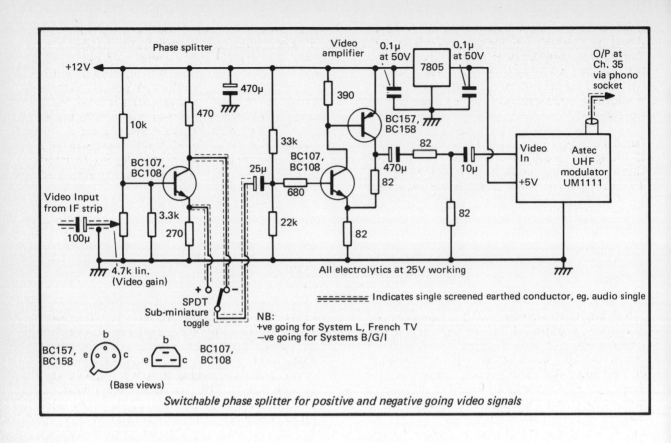

Switchable phase splitter for positive and negative going video signals

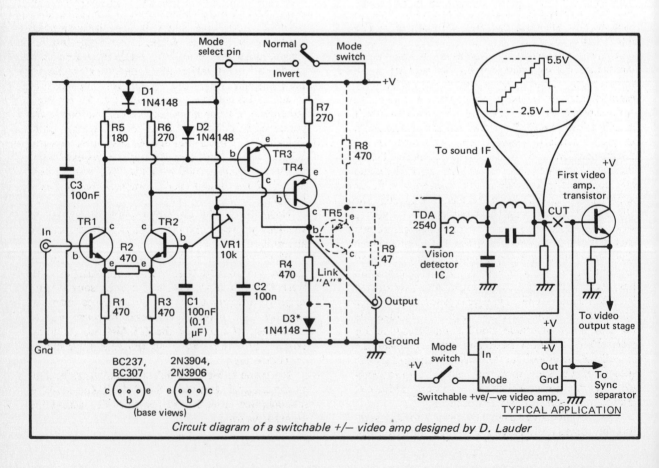

Circuit diagram of a switchable +/− video amp designed by D. Lauder

(fully clockwise) the voltage on the OUTPUT pin should be 0 V (+0.7 V for the buffered version). Turning VR1 anti-clockwise should have no effect initially then the output voltage should start to rise until it reaches 60% of the supply voltage then it should start to fall slightly. Remove the bias resistors from the INPUT.

Installation – General

If fitting the circuit to a 'live chassis' TV set no circuitry or wiring should be accessible outside the TV and the Mode switch should have a nylon shaft and no metal parts which are accessible outside the TV case. Portable TVs which work on mains or 12 volts DC generally have an isolated chassis and do not present such a hazard. If in doubt, seek advice.

The positive supply to the circuit should be taken from a point whose voltage does not drop significantly due to the extra current drawn. VR1 should initially be set fully clockwise then adjusted so that the voltage on the OUTPUT pin, when receiving a signal, does not change when switching to Invert mode. Great care is required if making this adjustment on a 'live chassis' TV.

COLOUR RECEPTION

Colour broadcasts are now being transmitted regularly in many countries. It is possible to receive such transmissions over long distances for both Tropospheric and Sporadic E propagation. By the nature of the transmission itself successful colour reception demands a higher standard of receiver efficiency if satisfactory colour signals are to be displayed. A number of colour systems are in use. PAL, SECAM and NTSC. The first two types are used in Europe, PAL by Western Europe excluding France, and SECAM in Eastern Europe and France. NTSC is used in the Americas and areas with the FCC 525 line system.

Unlike monochrome reception where video bandwidth can be sacrificed in the interests of an improved signal/noise figure and IF selectivity, it is essential that the IF strip retains the full bandwidth and response as laid down in the manufacturer's specification. Similarly it is essential that the aerial in use maintains a level response throughout the design bandwidth since the colour subcarrier lies at the high frequency end of the channel, if the aerial has been peaked to the vision frequency with an appropriate fall-off in performance towards the HF end difficulty may be experienced in locking weak long distance signals. Experience has shown that it is possible to reduce IF bandwidth to a degree that will prevent adjacent channel interference and retain normal colour operation. Such modification has been carried out by an experienced technician in the Arabian Gulf area to reduce interference problems and with excellent results. It is advisable however to avoid undue modification to any colour receiver's IF strip and associated circuitry unless one is fully experienced in television engineering, the success of any such work will depend on the versatility of the receiver's design to accept additional alteration in a critical part of the circuit.

The chrominance/luminance ratio should therefore be maintained, preferably with a variation not exceeding 6 dB, considering that the video bandwidth may be adversely affected in propagation.

The signal levels at which colour will 'lock' depend mainly on the efficiency of the colour killer circuitry, but it should be possible to obtain a colour lock simultaneously with normal synchronisation. Disabling the colour killer does help to receive weak signals in colour. This can normally be done by shorting out two appropriate test points or shorting a particular test point to chassis – the manual should be consulted for such adjustment. If the colour killer is left disabled colour noise will be displayed when receiving monochrome pictures. It is suggested that some arrangement be made to switch the colour killer 'in or out' of operation in the method as indicated. Experience has shown that colour signals by Sporadic E and Tropospheric propagation can be received, although the former mode is more difficult due to the continually fluctuating nature of the signal. Both SECAM and PAL colour signals have been received in the United Kingdom, although it appears easier to obtain a colour lock with the PAL system, as it has a simpler ident signal enabling lower signal working.

Noise on a SECAM signal tends to appear as streaking whereas noise with PAL has a finer speckled appearance.

When operating a PAL colour receiver in the United Kingdom (6 MHz sound/vision spacing) with West European PAL signals (5.5 MHz sound/vision spacing), patterning on the chrominance information has been noticed with some receivers, due to insufficient rejection of the 5.5 MHz sound intercarrier. In such a case extra IF sound traps should be incorporated.

In general terms for satisfactory colour reception, an input signal level some 8–10 dB higher than for monochrome reception is necessary for acceptable domestic viewing.

With increasing use of VCR equipment and availability of VCR tapes at competitive prices there is every reason to exploit the medium to improve results in the DX-TV field. The main advantage is of course the replay facility and distant signals can be recorded and played back to review specific sightings be they of exotic reception or of unidentified test patterns or captions. In the latter context the 'freeze frame' facility that is available on VCR machines will enable an unknown pattern to be examined frame by frame and in the hope of noting some form of identification. A signal incoming directly that suffers poor synchronisation can often be improved by recording onto tape and playing back through the VCR system. If an enthusiast has access to a 2nd compatible VCR machine it is possible to dub off sections of wanted video onto a 2nd cassette and to build up a complete library of test card and other DX video information. Such recordings are invaluable when demonstrating the art of TV-DXing to the layman, or for playing back for one's own satisfaction during the cheerless days of Winter!

Multi-standard PAL/SECAM/NTSC VCRs with appropriate sound spacing variations and incorporating VHF/UHF tuning are available from the more specialised video dealers. Certain UK VCR are fitted with VHF/UHF tuners which can be used as a basic (though perhaps inconvenient) Band 1/3 DXing receiver, outputting at the usual ch.36 into the main domestic TV receiver. If the domestic machine in use is a VHF/UHF type then this would allow for an inexpensive commencement into TV-DXing

— requiring only a Band 1 aerial. Operationally the tuning arrangements may be found inconvenient (unless remote scan tuning is featured) and in the long term a more efficient and dedicated receiving system should be aimed for. VCR machines do not convert standards and a monitor/receiver with appropriate systems/colour demodulating circuits will still be needed.

Many of the more specialised multi-standard system TV receivers have facilities for baseband video/audio outputs. These baseband signal feeds may be recorded onto a standard System I UK (UHF only) video recorder and then played back to a System I receiver (either the original multi-standard receiver) or another UK standard TV. Perfect mono vision and sound should be resolved on both types of receiver. For display of colour the playback TV must suit the incoming (original) signal standard, i.e. if for example the received signal was System D SECAM then a suitable SECAM receiver/monitor must be used for correct colour display. An incoming PAL signal will similarly require a PAL receiver/monitor and in this instance both the multi-standard system and the UK single standard TV should resolve colour. It will be understood that a French System L signal fed from the baseband outputs of a multi-standard TV (which includes System L capability) can be recorded on a UK standard VCR (via its video/audio input sockets) and then played back onto a System I UK standard TV with good mono vision and sound.

IMPORTED DUAL STANDARD TELEVISION RECEIVERS

For the non-technical TV enthusiast the attraction of the imported dual standard receiver for DXing use is considerable. This type of receiver, often with a relatively small screen, incorporates both VHF and UHF tuners, usually varicap tuned — and features intercarrier sound IF switching from the System I UK standard to System B/G West European standard, being 6 MHz and 5.5 MHz respectively. One problem that can arise, particularly if sited near to a Band 1 transmitter is that the latter signal — if strong — can 'spread' over a considerable part of the useable spectrum and prevent operation on one or more potential DX channels. The 'spread' is caused by the relatively wide response of the receiver's IF strip, and short of modification internally the only method of reducing the problem is with the use of notch

filters to remove the offending local transmissions. The problem may occur if for example strong signals are received on such a receiver via Sporadic E propagated signals on the adjacent channels E2 and R1. Due to the IF characteristics the 2 signals will tend to superimpose onto each other and with no means of increasing IF selectivity there is little that can be done. It may be possible to ease the problem somewhat with the use of a variable tuned notch filter and with the multiplicity of channels within the Band 1 spectrum a varicap tuned filter will prove operationally efficient. The design of such a filter is given within the 'Interference' section later in this volume.

Specialised UK dealers can supply multi-standard TVs that will resolve both PAL and SECAM (the latter for Systems D or L) colour and with variable sound options for B/G, D, I and L, or selections thereof. In general terms Far Eastern TVs rarely incorporate System L though at least 2 Scandinavian manufacturers (Luxor (UK) at Slough and Salora (UK) at Swindon) offer a 'building block' capability allowing the incorporation of various system modules as required – including Teletext and NTSC operation – and with 4 GHz/FM video options now or later for satellite reception, such 'upmarket' TVs normally are supplied with infra-red remote control and for TV-DXing purposes tend to be expensive.

SATELLITE TELEVISION TRANSMISSIONS

A veteran TV-DX enthusiast with considerable experience of satellite reception technology once commented that 'TV-DX is an art whereas satellite reception is a science'. TV-DX by definition is TV reception over a long distance, and although satellite TV downlink reception matches this definition opinion differs whether this is 'real' TV-DX. Before satellite TV downlinks were available, distant TV signals arrived by propagation enhancement, i.e. they were not normally present on a normal daily reception basis. By exploiting propagation phenomena, receiver and aerial techniques – and with an individual's experience – so these distant signals were received. The geosynchronous satellite at 36,000 km height is a line of sight source – if it's above the horizon it can (generally) be received – if it is below the horizon it can't! The ability to receive that signal relates to specific hardware; a dish, LNA, LNC, and a specialised receiver. Components for microwave use are precision made and reflect high cost. Much can be home constructed given the necessary skills. The following pages comprise a generalised section on satellites. References to past articles are given for very detailed construction of equipment and these should be available as back issues from the publisher or in bound form from a reference library suitable for photocopying. TVRO technology dates quickly but the information in these past articles should give clear guidance as to basic techniques and requirements.

By the mid-1980's direct broadcasting by satellite (DBS) still had not commenced in Europe though during 1986/7 a French/West German project should possibly be in service within the allocated 12 GHz band. Progress has unfortunately been slow, dogged with political and financial/funding discussion. With the lack of a positive move into DBS so manufacturers have maintained a watching and low development brief rather than an intensive development programme into 'domestic priced TVRO technology' (TVRO = TV Receive Only). As a result equipment that is available for the 11 GHz and upwards spectrum tends to reflect a rather high pricing structure, being generally produced on a 'one-off' basis for a very small commercial market, that is to say mainly cable companies, educational establishments and exiled UK citizens living in warmer parts of Western Europe seeking English language programming. At the time of writing, Taiwan manufactured 11 GHz equipment is just entering the UK market.

RF GaAsfet technology has advanced to the extent that cable TV programming downlinks within the 10.9–12.5 GHz band originally intended for +2 metre dishes can be received with adequate quality on dishes down to 1 metre within the domestic environment. The smaller size of dish allows the dedicated enthusiast to attempt 11 GHz reception without the environmental and financial problems of large dishes and at the time of writing 'kits' are available to further minimise front end electronics construction, though low noise devices still tend to be rather expensive.

A range of commercial dishes for the 10.9–12.5 GHz spectrum (SAT-TEL, Northampton)

The 3.675–4.2 GHz satellite allocation traditionally is the band for initiation into the mystique of satellite technology. Although larger dishes (1.8 metre is a minimum) are necessary for any attempt at acceptable reception, the one exception is Gorizont (14°W) which can provide noise-free reception down to a 1 metre dish on its 3.675 MHz Eurobeam. Gorizont carries the Russian 1st programme intended for TV relay in Eastern European countries, army camps, etc., and it provides the ideal source for constructing and testing a home engineered terminal.

Much pioneering work has been carried out by

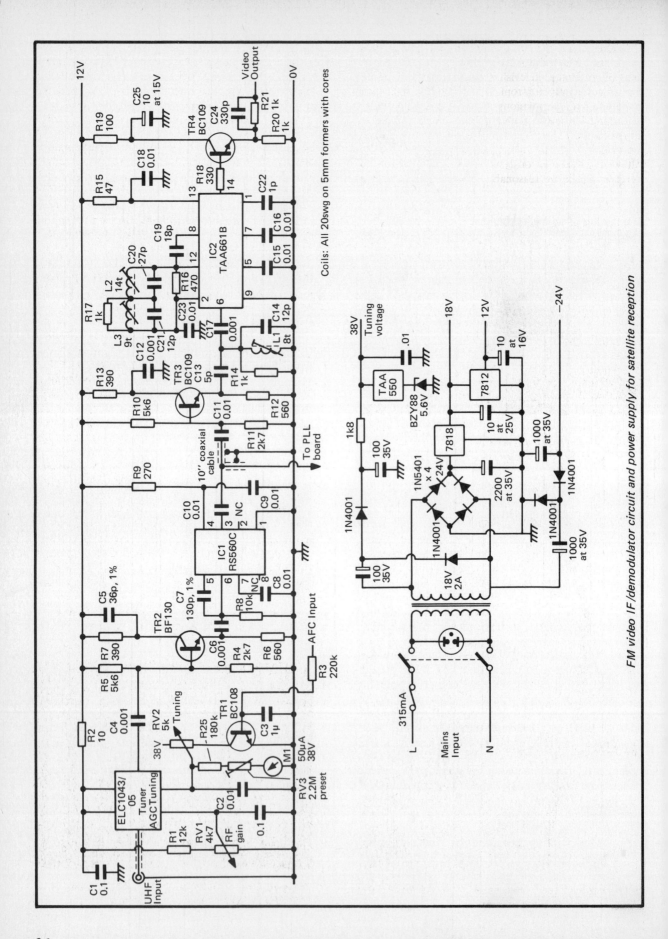

FM video IF/demodulator circuit and power supply for satellite reception

TV-DXers. Perhaps the most exciting project was ATS. In 1975/6 the ATS-6 'Site' experiment involving instructional television programming for the Indian sub-continent from its orbit at 35°E was most successful. Transmissions were at 860 MHz using wideband FM video modulation and with two sound channels. Despite the main signal beam being fixed on central India sufficient radiation 'off-beam' allowed several enthusiasts in Western Europe to receive signals of reasonable quality and on home

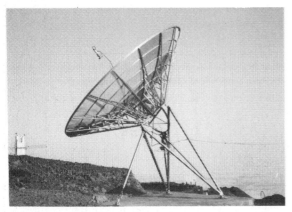

A 5-metre dish atop a mountain at La Palma, Canary Islands receiving the 4 GHz downlinks from SATCOM IV 83°W (Harrison Electronics, March, Cambs.)

constructed equipment. The USSR has at least one UHF direct broadcasting satellite (Statsionar T—Ekran) operating at 714—722 MHz and providing television for Northern Russia. Despite the 99° East position of the satellite, sufficient radiation due to characteristics of the transmitting aerial exists to enable experimenters as far distant as South Africa to resolve weak signals on relatively simple domestic equipment when using high gain receiving aerials. The future of direct satellite broadcasting, certainly for Europe will lie in the 12 GHz band. The Canadian CTS transmissions and later BSE transmissions for the Japanese islands have demonstrated that direct transmissions are capable of giving excellent results. Towards the end of 1978 the experimental OTS satellite was successfully orbited and commenced a series of low power test transmissions. It is to the credit and patience of at least one TV enthusiast that he successfully constructed an 11.6 GHz receiver to display good quality video.

The 12 GHz head and dish system are such that extreme precision is necessary in its construction. It is likely therefore that the enthusiast will be unable to produce his own head system. Furthermore it seems that there will be available mass produced 12 GHz head units when direct satellite broadcasting to Europe commences. The enthusiast can however construct much of the receiving equipment and proven circuitry is included within this section. The 12 GHz head unit will give wideband conversion to the 1st IF, this within the UHF band and the scope of conventional domestic UHF tuners. It is therefore possible to feed the IF output of a suitably tuned UHF tuner into the Phase Lock Loop demodulation circuit as shown, though IF output bandwidth may need further widening. The AM video output can then be fed into a conventional video monitor or remodulated back to VHF (or UHF) and into the normal domestic TV receiver.

As already mentioned several enthusiasts received pictures from ATS-6 and examples are shown together with details of equipment used. A 5 foot

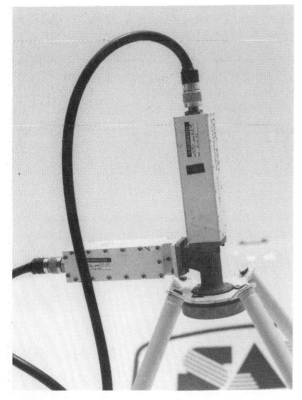

Dual polarisation (linear) 11 GHz feedhorn/LNA assembly (SAT-TEL)

Transmissions received from the ATS-6 satellite at 860 MHz in 1976 at Sheffield, England

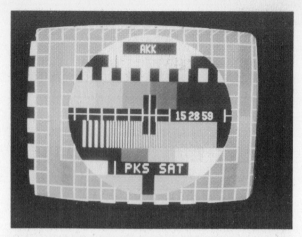

PKS test card with top vertical bending, an effect of PCM sound in syncs

Home constructed helical aerial for Ekran/Stat-T 714 MHz by TV-DXer in Sri Lanka

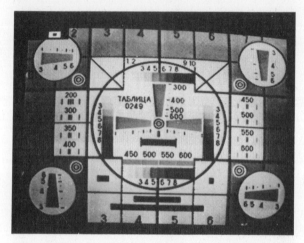

The USSR monoscope 0249 test card via the Gorizont 7 Spot beam at 3.675 GHz

PKS (German cable programme) on Eutelsat I-F1 11.507 GHz downlink

Twice a year the sun passes directly behind a geo-stationary satellite. The receiving dish 'sees' the sun as high level interference and is sufficient to wipe out normal downlink programming. Warnings are therefore carried detailing a 'Solar Outage' — such as this example on the WOLD downlink.

LIVE STUDIO FEED TO ABC FROM JCS JERUSALEM

Outside broadcast/studio links are often seen at 4 GHz such as the above example received at Denver, Colorado intended for ABC-TV.

HOUSE OF COMMONS
PROCEEDINGS RESUME
NOV 19/84 AT:

08:00 PACIFIC TIME
09:00 MOUNTAIN TIME
10:00 CENTRAL TIME
11:00 EASTERN TIME
12:00 ATLANTIC TIME
12:30 NFLD TIME

THIS IS THE CBC PARLIAMENTARY
TELEVISION NETWORK

The wide coverage from a single satellite downlink is shown on this Anik D downlink transmission covering the whole North American land mass.

diameter dish, fabricated in 12 sectors of ¼ inch expanded aluminium mesh and with a 22½ inch focal length. The driven element is a tuned circular quad element fed for vertical polarisation, spaced at ¼ wave from a ½ wave diameter copper disc reflector. A 2 stage transistor head amp (18 dB gain, 3 dB noise) is fitted to rear of the reflector. Coaxial cable feeds the UHF signal to the receiving equipment comprising a standard varicap UHF tuner into the circuit similar to that shown but with an additional PLL. One loop with a 3 MHz lock range feeds video to a monitor, the 2nd loop with only 500 KHz lock range explores sync tips and feeds sync information to the same monitor. An improvement of 3 dB noise bandwidth was obtained and enhanced sync

locking resulted by using the two independent loops. The precision required at 12 GHz is such that no details will be given for head construction. For the enthusiast that considers himself qualified to attempt such construction he would be advised to study the RSGB publication *VHF-UHF Manual* by D. S. Evans and G. R. Jessop, and the various articles detailed at the end of this section.

Any form of satellite reception on a line of sight path will involve a free space path loss over the circuit — this signal loss will vary according to the frequency in use and the path length involved. Tables are available in communication handbooks detailing such path losses. A further problem occurs in the avoidance of polarisation shift — this would happen to a plane polarised signal over a long path — the signal is transmitted circularly polarised. For optimum reception results a helical aerial is required to match the incoming wavefront which may be either clockwise or anti-clockwise polarised. It is possible to use crossed Yagis for this purpose, reversal of polarisation screw being achieved by switching specific lengths of cable into the aerial feeders. Experience suggests that the polarisation rotation problem is greatly reduced at frequencies above 1 GHz (1,000 MHz). Generally the use of a dish parabola is advised above 1 GHz whereas below this figure the gain of a parabola is such that stacked Yagis will give a greater gain and cleaner polar diagram.

The construction of an accurate dish should present little problem to the dedicated enthusiast. Information and dimensions are given in a number of amateur radio handbooks devoted to microwave activities. A dish for UHF reception can be constructed using ½ inch mesh chicken netting — for maximum efficiency this dimension should not be exceeded. Fibre glass and aluminium foil offer other possibilities and copper pipe can be used in the construction of circular polarisation feed elements.

It is unlikely that a great expansion in UHF DBS will occur, though Ekran will continue for some years since it allows direct reception on relatively simple aerial receiving equipment over the vast tract of Northern Russia. Both India and the Arab States have opted for the 2.6 GHz band with community TV downlinking via INSAT and ARABSAT craft respectively. UHF would typically feature a beamwidth of between $7°-10°$ in covering large areas — such as India; for transmission to individual countries in Europe a beamwidth between $0.5°-1.5°$ will be employed and operating within the selected band 11.7–12.5 GHz (11,700–12,500 MHz). Due to power considerations wide band frequency modulation is the most likely system to be adopted having a peak-to-peak deviation of approximately 16 MHz and a channel bandwidth of 24 MHz.

Receiving aerials will vary between the traditional parabolic dish and newly developed planar arrays printed onto copper clad laminates. For sufficient gain the aperture of the dish system will be approximately one metre and the aperture of the laminated array will need to be approaching 1.6 m.square for an equivalent gain figure. Due to the high losses at such frequencies the incoming 12 GHz signals will be downconverted adjacent to the aerial system with further conversion at the receiver to video and remodulated to either VHF or UHF AM video. NHK, Tokyo have perfected a design that gives direct to AM video downconverted to UHF or VHF at the head itself with a system noise figure of below 4.5 dB. It is anticipated that this design will become available for mass production of low cost domestic satellite receivers.

Currently considerable research is taking place with a view to evolving new reception techniques at these frequencies which will inevitably bring improvements in aerials and conversion methods.

The following back copies of 'Television' (IPC Magazines) should be consulted for detailed constructional data at 4 GHz: *November 1982 – Feedhorn construction and downconverter; May 1983 – 4 GHz downconverter; September 1983 – Low Noise 4 GHz amplifier with helical feed; October 1983/January 1984 incl. – Complete series on receiver construction.* Detailed construction at 11 GHz: *February 1985 – Low noise 11 GHz converter; July 1985 – 11 GHz Low Noise Amplifier (LNA).* A new TVRO receiver by John Wood, CQ-TV No. 135 (BATC), detailed project for an IF input (950–1450 MHz) TVRO receiver, video and audio PCBs and components available.

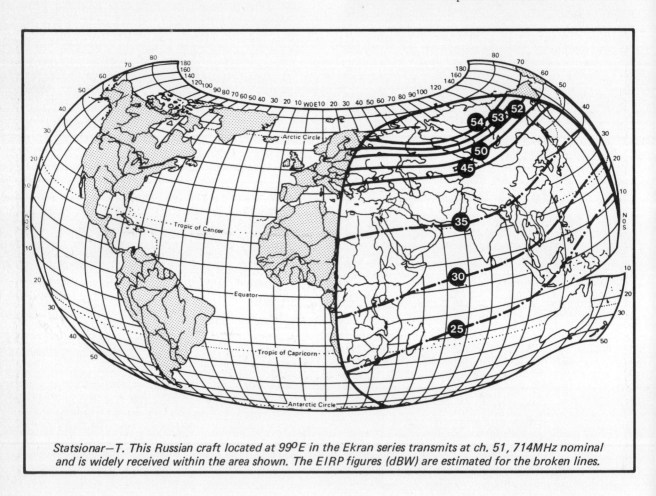

Statsionar–T. This Russian craft located at 99°E in the Ekran series transmits at ch. 51, 714MHz nominal and is widely received within the area shown. The EIRP figures (dBW) are estimated for the broken lines.

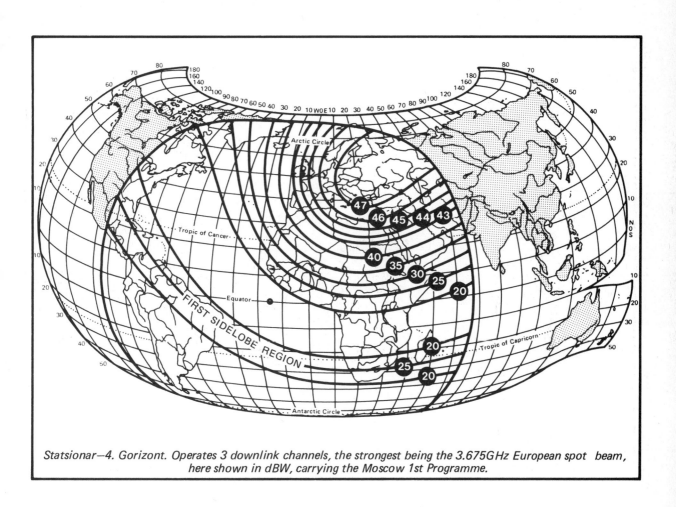

Statsionar—4. Gorizont. Operates 3 downlink channels, the strongest being the 3.675GHz European spot beam, here shown in dBW, carrying the Moscow 1st Programme.

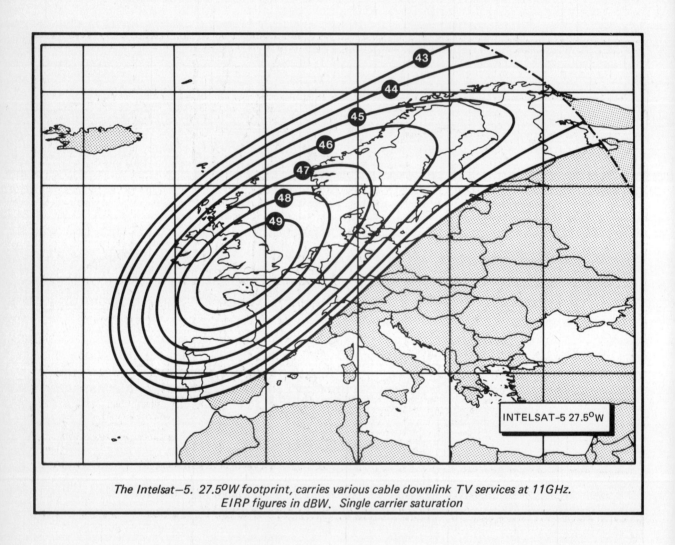

The Intelsat—5. 27.5ºW footprint, carries various cable downlink TV services at 11GHz.
EIRP figures in dBW. Single carrier saturation

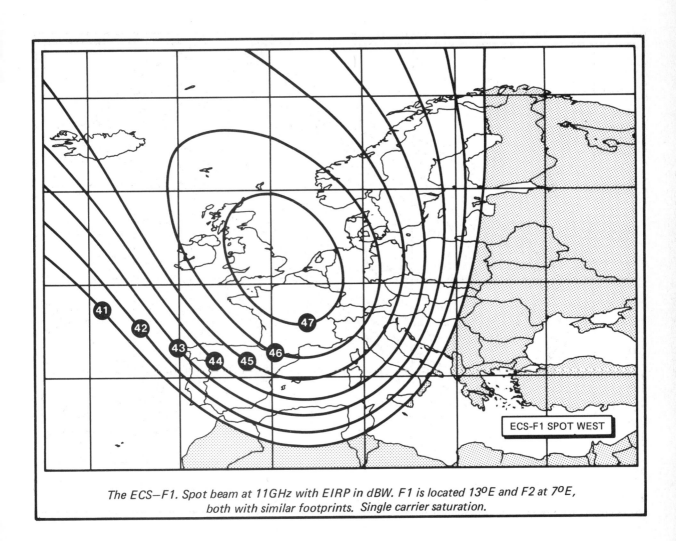

The ECS—F1. Spot beam at 11GHz with EIRP in dBW. F1 is located 13ºE and F2 at 7ºE, both with similar footprints. Single carrier saturation.

SATELLITE BROADCASTING FREQUENCY BANDS

12 GHz European Channel Allocation

	Channels	Polarisation	Orbital Position (Degrees)
Hungary	22 26 30 34 38	1	−1
Poland	1 5 9 13 17	2	−1
East Germany	21 25 29 33 37	2	−1
Czechoslovakia	3 7 11 15 19	2	−1
Bulgaria	4 8 12 16 20	1	−1
Rumania	2 6 10 14 18	1	−1
Denmark	12 16 20	2	5
Denmark (Nordic Area)	24 36	2	5
Finland	2 6 10	2	5
Finland (Nordic Area)	22 26	2	5
Sweden	4 8 34	2	5
Sweden (Nordic Area)	30 40	2	5
Norway	14 18 38	2	5
Norway (Nordic Area)	28 32	2	5
Greece	3 7 11 15 19	1	5
Yugoslavia	21 25 29 33 37 23 27 31 35 39	1	−7
France	1 5 9 13 17	1	−19
West Germany	2 6 10 14 18	2	−19
Italy	24 28 32 36 40	2	−19
Luxembourg	3 7 11 15 19	1	−19
Belgium	21 25 29 33 37	1	−19
Netherlands	23 27 31 35 39	1	−19
Austria	4 8 12 16 20	2	−19
Switzerland	22 26 30 34 38	2	−19
United Kingdom	4 8 12 16 20	1	−31
Ireland	2 6 10 14 18	1	−31
Portugal	3 7 11 15 19	2	−31
Spain	23 27 31 35 39	2	−31
Liechtenstein	3 7 11 15 19	1	−37
Andorra	4 8 12 16 20	2	−37
Monaco	21 25 29 33 27	1	−37
San Marino	1 5 9 13 17	1	−37
Vatican City	23 27 31 35 39	1	−37

Polarisation: 1 Left-hand Circular
                    2 Right-hand Circular
EIRP: Generally range 1½ to 8 MW

Frequency Bands Allocated for Satellite Broadcasting (Region 1 — Europe, Africa, USSR)

620–790 MHz	Allocated to the broadcasting services and may be assigned to satellites for Frequency Modulation television subject to administrative and technical agreement.
2.5–2.69 GHz	Allocated to the broadcasting satellite service and to the fixed and mobile services. Satellite use is restricted to national and regional programmes — subject to agreement as above.
11.7–12.5 GHz	Allocated to the satellite broadcasting service and to fixed and mobile services.
41–43 GHz	Allocated to the satellite broadcasting service.
84–86 GHz	Allocated to the satellite broadcasting service.

Transmission for the European area will be within the 11.7–12.5 GHz spectrum.

Frequency Bands being used for telecommunications/ TV cable programming in the European Region

3.675–4.2 GHz	Allocated for telecommunications though TV downlinks are received with suitable equipment.
10.9–11.6 GHz	Allocated for telecommunications with TV programming available for cable systems though capable of 'home' reception with suitable equipment. Scrambling/ encryption of both video and audio may be encountered.

Channel Numbers and Assigned Frequencies for the 12 GHz Satellite Broadcasting Band (MHz)

1	11727.48	15	11996.00	29	12264.52
2	11746.66	16	12015.18	30	12283.70
3	11765.84	17	12034.36	31	12302.88
4	11785.02	18	12053.54	32	12322.06
5	11804.20	19	12072.72	33	12341.24
6	11823.38	20	12091.90	34	12360.42
7	11842.56	21	12111.08	35	12379.60
8	11861.74	22	12130.26	36	12398.78
9	11880.92	23	12149.44	37	12417.96
10	11900.10	24	12168.62	38	12437.14
11	11919.28	25	12187.80	39	12456.32
12	11938.46	26	12206.98	40	12475.50
13	11957.64	27	12226.16		
14	11976.82	28	12245.34		

Note: UK channels 4, 8, 12, 16 & 20 orbit position 31°W.

Proposed Broadcast Satellite Parameters for the Frequency Band 11.7–12.5 GHz

Type of modulation	fm	
Number of lines	625	
Sound sub-carrier frequency	6 MHz	
Peak-peak deviation	13.3 MHz	
Peak deviation of sound sub-carrier	50 kHz	
Receiver equivalent rectangular noise bandwidth	27 MHz	
Angle of elevation	15°	40°
Luminance signal — unweighted noise for 99% of worst month	34 dB	33 dB
Sound signal to weighted noise ratio for 99% of worst month	51 dB	50 dB

Channel Allocations at 4 GHz

North American domestic satellite receiving equipment is normally calibrated by transponder number from 1 through to 24, covering 3.7 to 4.2 GHz. Most Domsats currently operational carry 24 transponder capability.

The two tables show frequency allocation for 12 and 24 channel working practice. Reversed polarisation operation on adjacent channels in 24 transponder is to give additional protection against adjacent channel interference.

Transponder assignments for 12 channel satellite are as follows (all horizontally polarised):

Transponder number	Downlink band	Channel centre frequency
1	3702–3738 MHz	3720 MHz
2	3742–3778 MHz	3760 MHz
3	3782–3818 MHz	3800 MHz
4	3822–3858 MHz	3840 MHz
5	3862–3898 MHz	3880 MHz
6	3902–3938 MHz	3920 MHz
7	3942–3978 MHz	3960 MHz
8	3982–4018 MHz	4000 MHz
9	4022–4058 MHz	4040 MHz
10	4062–4098 MHz	4080 MHz
11	4102–4138 MHz	4120 MHz
12	4142–4178 MHz	4160 MHz

Transponder assignments for 24 channel satellites are horizontally polarised for the even numbered transponders and vertically polarised for the odd numbered transponders:

Transponder number	Downlink band	Channel centre frequency
1 (V)	3702–3738 MHz	3720 MHz
2 (H)	3722–3758 MHz	3740 MHz
3 (V)	3742–3778 MHz	3760 MHz
4 (H)	3762–3798 MHz	3780 MHz
5 (V)	3782–3818 MHz	3800 MHz
6 (H)	3802–3838 MHz	3820 MHz
7 (V)	3822–3858 MHz	3840 MHz
8 (H)	3842–3878 MHz	3860 MHz
9 (V)	3862–3898 MHz	3880 MHz
10 (H)	3882–3918 MHz	3900 MHz
11 (V)	3902–3938 MHz	3920 MHz
12 (H)	3922–3958 MHz	3940 MHz
13 (V)	3942–3978 MHz	3960 MHz
14 (H)	3962–3998 MHz	3980 MHz
15 (V)	3982–4018 MHz	4000 MHz
16 (H)	4002–4038 MHz	4020 MHz
17 (V)	4022–4058 MHz	4040 MHz
18 (H)	4042–4078 MHz	4060 MHz
19 (V)	4062–4098 MHz	4080 MHz
20 (H)	4082–4118 MHz	4100 MHz
21 (V)	4102–4138 MHz	4120 MHz
22 (H)	4122–4158 MHz	4140 MHz
23 (V)	4142–4178 MHz	4160 MHz
24 (H)	4162–4198 MHz	4180 MHz

GLOSSARY OF SATELLITE TV TERMS

A

Aperture — the 'square area' or size of the parabolic dish aerial.

Audio Subcarrier — a satellite downlink may feature one or more audio subcarriers within the 5–8 MHz range, allowing for stereo, multiple language sound channels etc. The satellite receiver usually features an 'Audio Tune' control to allow independent tuning of these discrete carriers.

Az/El Mount — a dish support structure that allows for adjustment separately in both azimuth and elevation.

Azimuth — the horizontal rotation of a receiving dish expressed as a compass bearing relative to true North and measured in a clockwise direction.

B

Beamwidth — the polar diagram of a dish aerial indicating the 'narrowness' of the main forward pickup lobe, with increasing gain so the beamwidth reduces as indeed does the beamwidth reduce with increasing frequency. The gain of a dish aerial is usually expressed in dBi (dB Isotropic), a given dish size will have an increasing gain with frequency.

Boresight — that part on the Earth's surface to which the transmitting satellite aerial is aimed and where the strongest field strength (dBw) will be encountered.

C

C Band — the TV satellite band 3.7–4.2 GHz, in extensive use over North America with 1.2 million TVRO terminals in home use as of time of writing.

C/N — carrier-to-noise ratio, when used with TVRO compares the satellite downlink carrier strength with the received noise level after the LNA (in dB).

Cassegrain Aerial — a secondary reflective system in

which a main reflector dish has a hyperbolic sub-reflector mounted at the focal point, the latter concentrating the signal back to the centre of the main dish where the feedhorn system is positioned.

Circular Polarisation — Intelsat and other tele-communication satellites use circular polarisation, either left hand, right hand or a mixture of both.

Clarke Belt — the orbital belt some 22,300 miles above the Earth where geostationary satellites are slotted.

D

Dish Efficiency — performance figure of a dish aerial in respect to gain, usually in the 60—65% region though claims of 70% efficiency for parabolic dishes have been made in the USA.

Dish Illumination — the part of the dish aerial as 'seen' by the feedhorn, care must be taken in the feedhorn design to ensure for a given F/D design that the feed when positioned at the focal point doesn't see too much off the dish edge or doesn't see enough of the dish surface.

Downlink — the satellite transmitted signal down to the Earth's surface.

Dual Feedhorn — a feedhorn that features two inte-grated waveguide systems allowing operation in two bands (e.g. C Band and Ku Band). Seperate headend electronics will be necessary though with a common IF output spectrum allowing for a diplexed feed into a common receiver downfeeder.

Dual Orthomode Coupler — a waveguide mounted feed system allowing the reception of both horizon-tal and vertically polarised downlink signals. Adjacent downlink channels on domestic satellites in the USA reverse polarity to minimise adjacent channel inter-ference.

E

EIRP — effective isotropic radiated power is a measure of the signal strength transmitted towards the Earth.

Elevation — the vertical movement of a receiving dish expressed in degrees above the horizon.

F

F/D Ratio — an indication of the depth of a dish and is calculated by dividing the focal length by the diameter, a higher ratio means a shallower dish.

Feed — the signal collecting components — usually the feedhorn with its mechanical supporting structure located at the focal point.

Feedhorn — a single band device that concentrates the downlink signals at the focal point, channels them into a waveguide and to the first active stages — usually the LNA.

Focal Length — the distance from the feed point (focal point) to the centre of the dish.

Footprint — the area of the Earth's surface the downlink is covering and shown as a contour map expressed in dBw. It is a good guide to the size of receiving aerial needed at any spot within that contour map.

G

G/T — a figure of merit utilising the characteristics of the aerial gain, LNA noise level and the surround-ing environment ambient noise — expressed in dB per 1 degree K. With an increasing G/T number so picture quality will improve.

K

Ku Band — the TV satellite band within the 11.7—12.6 GHz intended for use within the European area and already in limited use over North America (Anik series). The 10.9—11.7 GHz band in Europe is receiving an increasing interest with its cable downlink operations.

L

L.N.A. — low noise amplifier — the first wideband signal amplifying stages. Low noise operation is important to optimise system signal noise, usually measured in degrees Kelvin ($^{\circ}$K). Typical C band noise levels in LNAs are under 100°K with more upmarket LNAs down to 65°K. Found head mounted in a weatherproof metal case.

L.N.B. — a low noise block downconverter, accepts the LNA wideband output and downconverts the complete frequency block to an equivalent lower frequency IF bandwidth — this allows one or more receivers to be used in tuning across the first IF bandwidth.

L.N.C. — a combined weather sealed package of LNA and low noise downconverter.

L.N.F. — a combined feedhorn/LNA package.

Look Angle — the property of a given satellite aerial mount system to position (or look) towards the Clarke Belt.

N

Noise — degradation of a received signal due to insufficient input signal level — measured in $^{\circ}$K (noise temperature).

O

Offset Angle — the tilting (in degrees) of a polar mount aerial from its polar axis to ensure correct tracking (horizon to horizon) of geostationary satellites in the Clarke Belt, this angle increases the further North the receiving location is from the Equator (also called declination angle).

Offset Fed Aerial — a reflector action system in which the focal point is 'offset' or stood off to one side of the main reflector, thus no feed support blockage within the main reflector aperture occurs and improved efficiency results.

P

Parabolic Dish — an aerial with a specific (logarith-mic) curved surface to reflect all incident signals to a common (small) focal point on the central axis.

Polarisation — the transmitted downlink sense of a satellite signal which may be either vertical, horizontal or circular (left or right hand).

Polar Mount — a dish support structure that allows for simultaneous adjustment of both elevation and azimuth, often utilised for tracking the Clarke satellite belt.

Prime Focus Feed — a dish aerial in which the feedhorn/LNA assembly is mounted at the focal point.

S

Satellite Receiver — the channel tuning control unit that features video/audio tune, fine tune, polarity skew, AFC etc., etc., and with baseband or an RF modulated output. Will also supply head end electronics with power via the downfeeder.

Scalar Feed — several concentric rings aligned around the feedhorn mouth to optimise the feedhorn forward pickup lobe characteristics and is very commonly found in use with current designed TVRO systems.

Scrambling — deliberate 'distortion' (encoding) of the transmitted signal to prevent reception by an unauthorised viewer. A decoder is necessary to correct the 'distortion'. Various scrambling methods are currently in operation. Also known as 'encryption'.

Signal Threshold — the performance capabilities of a TVRO to produce minimal noise/noise-free signals (measured in dB).

Sparklies — degradation on a received satellite picture with small black/white dots/streaks — caused by insufficient signal (poor signal/noise ratio).

T

Transponder — an uplink receiver/amplifier/transmitter aboard a satellite which radiates a given channel on its downlink.

T.V.R.O. — Television receive only.

V

V.T.O. — a voltage tuned oscillator package used in either the receiver for tuning across the downconverted block IF, or used in earlier tuneable head downconverters, resulting in a single channel IF output.

AERIALS

The aerial is one of the most important sections of the receiving chain, as the signal voltage conveyed to the aerial input of the television receiver will determine the eventual quality of the image displayed upon the screen. Consequently every effort must be made to obtain the highest possible signal voltage.

The use of a wide band Band 1 aerial is advocated in later pages for successful TV-DXing and the UK enthusiast has the option of either constructing his own array or purchasing from several commercial types that have been made available specificly for the 'TV-DXer'. For Band 3 and higher commercial wide band arrays are commonly available and certainly due to the more exacting aerial requirements it is not advisable to construct one's own aerials for such frequencies. It is unlikely that a home constructed aerial would give the same degree of matching and performance over these wide bandwidths as would be encountered on a correctly designed array for Band 3 and above. In the Americas with the large number of transmitters in operation, wideband arrays are extensively used, it being not uncommon to encounter a single aerial covering ch.A2—A83 inclusive. Generally the enthusiast within this area will operate a wide band array covering VHF and another wide band array for UHF, unlike his European counterpart that uses separate aerials for each band. Certainly an improved performance must be expected when single band aerials are used and where possible this course is strongly advised.

The most simple aerial encountered for television reception is the half wave dipole. This comprises a single rod cut to the appropriate operating frequency. Such an aerial, vertically mounted, will be capable of receiving vertically polarised transmissions through a complete 360° arc and is termed as having an omni-directional receiving pattern. A half wave dipole mounted horizontally will receive horizontally polarised transmissions at maximum strength when the dipole is broadside to the signal path. Consequently there will be two main receiving lobes for such an aerial, at 180° to each other and if plotted on a circular scale will show a receiving pattern (polar diagram) shaped like a figure '8'. To calculate the length of a half wave receiving dipole at a given frequency the formula:

$$\frac{468}{\text{frequency (MHz)}}$$

will give the answer in feet.

This formula gives the electrical half wavelength as applied to an aerial structure and is shorter than the physical half wavelength in free space. The reason for this shortening factor is related to the velocity of propagation within the aerial structure, the effects of the aerial elements and its supporting insulation actually causes an incident wave to slow down. A further complication arises since the diameter of the aerial element is a related factor to be included in accurate calculation for correct resonance. For our purposes however it is sufficient to regard a correction factor of 5% as related to the free space half wavelength. To find the correct free space half wavelength the following formula may be used:

$$\frac{492}{f\ (MHz)} \quad \text{(answer in feet)}$$

In all calculations relating to aerial construction and element lengths the '468' formula must be used but to establish correct spacing between stacked arrays the '492' formula should be used. The velocity factor of some coaxial cables can be much higher than the 5% factor as noted above and in such cases the '492' formula should be used and multiplied by the velocity factor of the specified cable, e.g.:

$$\frac{492}{f\ (MHz)} \times 0.85 \quad \text{(answer in feet)}$$

This will give an electrical half wavelength of a section of coaxial cable having a velocity factor of 0.85.

The signal induced within the dipole is usually fed to the receiver by means of coaxial cable. The connection is made at the centre of the half wave dipole. At this point the characteristics impedance is in the order of 70–75 ohms and to ensure the minimum loss of signal a coaxial cable also having a characteristic impedance of 75 ohms should be used, thus ensuring a good match and the maximum

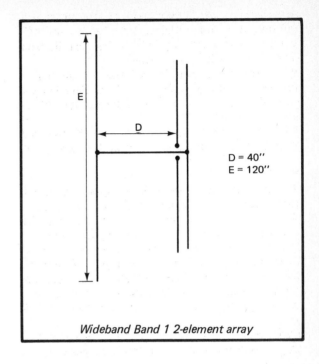

Wideband Band 1 2-element array

D = 40"
E = 120"

transfer of signal energy from the dipole into the cable. If there is a mismatch at this point a loss of signal will occur. In Europe and the Americas, ribbon feeder is commonly used with a somewhat higher impedance than the coaxial cable mentioned, and is connected to a dipole assembly having an appropriately higher centre impedance. The same general comments apply to this feeder as to coaxial cable.

The half wave dipole is satisfactory when operated in a field of high signal strength but enhanced gain is required when signal strengths fall to a low value. An improvement in gain can be obtained by mounting another longer element a distance from the dipole (usually ¼ to ½ wavelength spacing). This element reflects signals back to the dipole thus increasing the signal voltage within the dipole. Further elements, called directors, shorter than the dipole, can be mounted in front of the dipole and together with the reflector provides a considerable increase in signal gain. With the increasing number of elements so the polar diagram changes, from that of omni-directional (in the case of vertical polarisation), to one showing a forward lobe in one particular direction and with minimum responses in other directions. The sharpness of the main forward lobe will depend upon the number of elements within the aerial system. A horizontally polarised aerial will also show an enhanced forward pickup lobe when the elements are increased in number. Unfortunately when additional elements are added to an aerial system the centre impedance of the dipole will drop from the initial 75 ohms to a considerably lower figure. To maintain a good match to the cable, the dipole impedance may be again

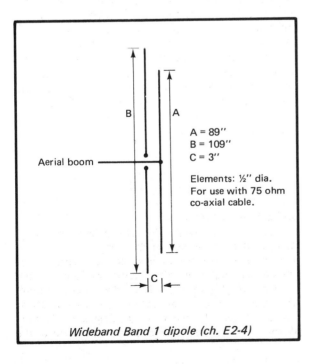

Aerial boom

A = 89"
B = 109"
C = 3"

Elements: ½" dia.
For use with 75 ohm co-axial cable.

Wideband Band 1 dipole (ch. E2-4)

increased by folding the dipole or by various other means. A typical array, designed for one channel, operation will have a bandwidth of approximately 5–7 MHz, this figure depending upon the frequency in use, the number of elements in the aerial array and the type and thickness of the dipole. An aerial having a reflector and a number of directors is known as a Yagi, the dipole being the active element, the other elements passive.

For the purpose of long distance television reception when a number of channels have to be covered efficiently, a wide band aerial should be used. The design of such an aerial follows a basic formula of tuning the various elements comprising the array to certain frequencies within the operating bandwidths. Usually the directors are tuned to the high frequency end, the dipole midway, and the reflector assembly to the lower frequency end of the band. If a number of directors are used this will tend to lift the gain at the high frequency end somewhat higher than that of the low frequency end. As signal losses tend to increase with frequency, the increased high frequency gain will tend to equal out such losses and give a more level response over the band.

Several Wide Band 1 designs are shown ranging from a simple dipole to more elaborate designs.

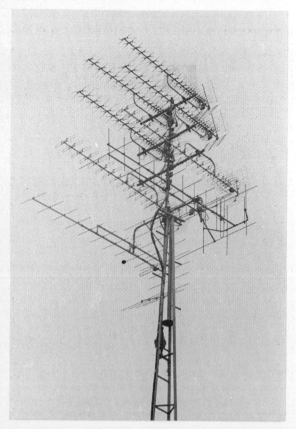

An elaborate TV-DXing aerial system for Band 3/UHF used by Ryn Muntjewerff (RMU) at Beemster, Holland

Three of the designs feature variations of the patented Antiference 'Tru-match' system in which the active dipole has a closely coupled passive dipole but cut to the high frequency part of the required bandwidth. The driven dipole being longer than half wave is inductive at the low frequency end whilst the parasitic dipole is less than half wave and so is capacitive at the high frequency end thus producing a better match over the design bandwidth. The action of the two dipoles produces at resonance a close match to 75 ohms and off resonance the reactive swings are reduced due to the self-correcting properties of each dipole element. The two element version gives a degree of forward gain over the bandwidth, the four element however gives increased gain particularly over the high frequency end of the band. A folded dipole is used for an improved feeder/aerial match since close spacing is used with the reflector and first director.

Jaybeam, one of the UK's foremost manufacturers of television aerials suggested another design for a three element wide band system which uses a single dipole only and incorporates an increased bandwidth reaching down to 40 MHz. The range of wide band Yagis is completed with the five element array based on the Jaybeam design but slightly modified for chs. E2–4 inclusive coverage. Band 2 (TV) dimensions are also given. For use with 300 ohms ribbon feeder the dipole should be folded giving a four times increase in impedance. At Band 3 and higher such wide band arrays prove easier to match accurately into the appropriate feeder and often small matching transformers (Baluns) are included.

A simple aerial which gives an omni-directional coverage is illustrated. This consists of two dipoles, cut to ch.E3 mounted at 90° to each other, phased and matched together into a 75 ohms output. The aerial when mounted horizontally provides a circular receiving pattern due to the combination of the 2 'figure of 8' polar diagrams of the dipoles. This aerial is recommended for Band 1 Meteor Shower/Scatter (MS) and Sporadic E use for the person unable to erect large arrays. This array may be constructed using the wide band dipole (Tru-match system) with an improved match over the chs. E2–4 bandwidth, rather than the straight single dipoles as shown. The matching and phasing harness remains unaltered. A commercial wide band ferrite cored combiner could be used to couple the 2 dipoles in place of the cable harness ensuring the 2 feeders to the transformer are of equal length.

Another type of array that has a superior performance for Band 1 reception is the Log Periodic due to a level gain throughout the design bandwidth, excellent matching, low VSWR and a very clean polar diagram free from minor lobes. The 6 element as shown features a director which can be omitted to reduce the overall boom length. Connections between each dipole can comprise copper cable

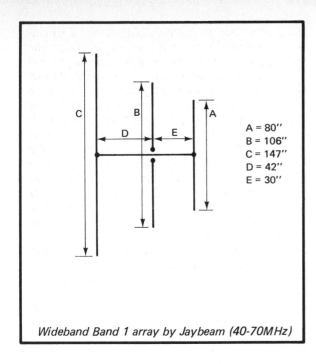

A = 80″
B = 106″
C = 147″
D = 42″
E = 30″

Wideband Band 1 array by Jaybeam (40-70MHz)

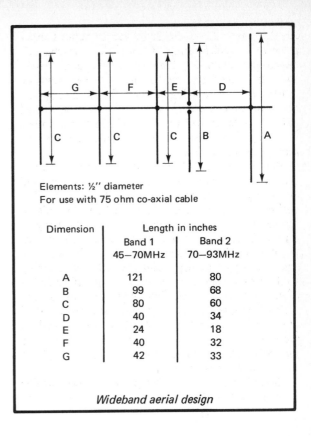

Elements: ½″ diameter
For use with 75 ohm co-axial cable

Dimension	Length in inches	
	Band 1 45—70MHz	Band 2 70—93MHz
A	121	80
B	99	68
C	80	60
D	40	34
E	24	18
F	40	32
G	42	33

Wideband aerial design

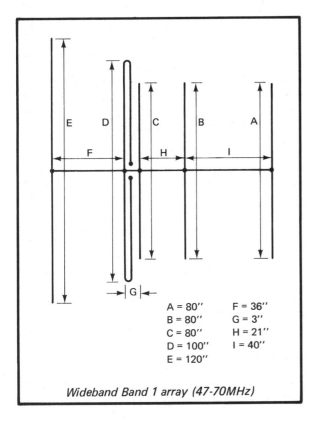

A = 80″   F = 36″
B = 80″   G = 3″
C = 80″   H = 21″
D = 100″   I = 40″
E = 120″

Wideband Band 1 array (47-70MHz)

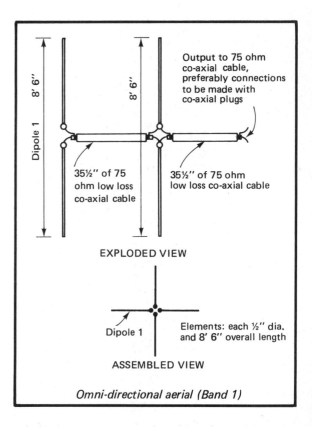

Output to 75 ohm co-axial cable, preferably connections to be made with co-axial plugs

35½″ of 75 ohm low loss co-axial cable

35½″ of 75 ohm low loss co-axial cable

Dipole 1 8′ 6″

8′ 6″

EXPLODED VIEW

Dipole 1

Elements: each ½″ dia. and 8′ 6″ overall length.

ASSEMBLED VIEW

Omni-directional aerial (Band 1)

51

soldered to tags on each dipole mounting. The tags and the immediate area on the dipole element must be greased (ideally silicone) in the interests of minimising electrolytic corrosion. The 75-ohm coaxial feeder should be either taped underneath the boom and for the total length to the rear or passed inside the actual boom element itself. Care should be taken to avoid the boom filling with water. This type of array is not the easiest to manufacture by the amateur enthusiast and the beginner into the hobby would be advised to initially concentrate on the simpler Yagi systems detailed earlier.

Wide band arrays for Band 3 and UHF are now commonly available, having high gain and an excellent performance generally. The field is so wide that the would-be purchaser is advised to contact the various manufacturers or suppliers for imformation. Within the UK several manufacturers produce Wide

A Band 1 TV-Dxing system with (lower) 2 element wideband and (upper) crossed wideband dipoles with crossed reflectors phased together and giving omni-directional coverage

Wideband Band 1 3-element array (Weston Developments)

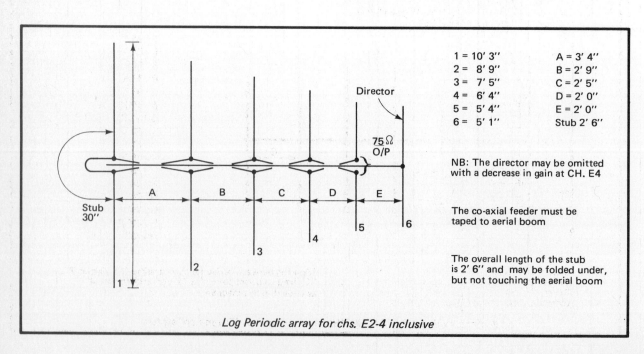

1 = 10' 3''   A = 3' 4''
2 = 8' 9''   B = 2' 9''
3 = 7' 5''   C = 2' 5''
4 = 6' 4''   D = 2' 0''
5 = 5' 4''   E = 2' 0''
6 = 5' 1''   Stub 2' 6''

NB: The director may be omitted with a decrease in gain at CH. E4

The co-axial feeder must be taped to aerial boom

The overall length of the stub is 2' 6'' and may be folded under, but not touching the aerial boom

Director

75 Ω O/P

Stub 30''

A   B   C   D   E

Log Periodic array for chs. E2-4 inclusive

Band 3 arrays, such as the J Beam 'Astrabeam', which is available in versions up to a double 11, possessing a high gain and a sharp forward pickup lobe.

With increasing activity at UHF competition between manufacturers has heralded greatly improved arrays departing somewhat from the conventional Yagi appearance with director assemblies following Continental European practice.

Several manufacturers currently produce versions of the multiple director unit array and although the appearance may differ somewhat the basic theory remains unaltered. The multiple director unit is an attempt to obtain the performance of a stacked array by supporting the director elements in a position that would be occupied by the individual directors of the separate stacked aerials. The advantage with the system is that a very high gain may be obtained using only one aerial boom and without the need for restricting cable harness, a gain that would be unobtainable from a conventional Yagi with straight director elements. Illustrations show the types of multiple director array now available in the United Kingdom.

The UHF transmitter coverage has been arranged

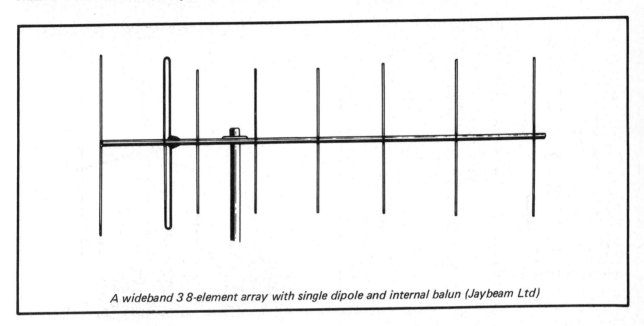

A wideband 3 8-element array with single dipole and internal balun (Jaybeam Ltd)

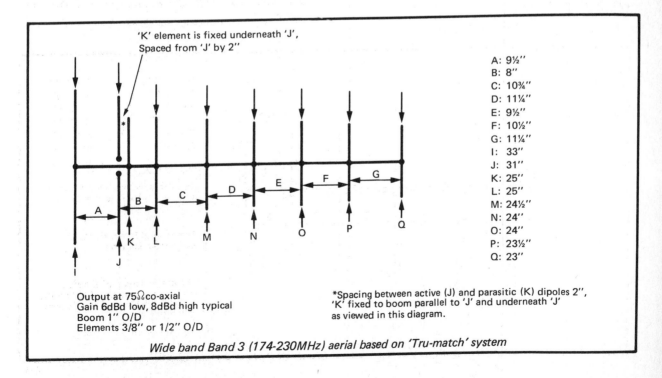

'K' element is fixed underneath 'J',
Spaced from 'J' by 2''

A: 9½''
B: 8''
C: 10¾''
D: 11¼''
E: 9½''
F: 10½''
G: 11¼''
I: 33''
J: 31''
K: 25''
L: 25''
M: 24½''
N: 24''
O: 24''
P: 23½''
Q: 23''

Output at 75Ω co-axial
Gain 6dBd low, 8dBd high typical
Boom 1'' O/D
Elements 3/8'' or 1/2'' O/D

*Spacing between active (J) and parasitic (K) dipoles 2'',
'K' fixed to boom parallel to 'J' and underneath 'J'
as viewed in this diagram.

Wide band Band 3 (174-230MHz) aerial based on 'Tru-match' system

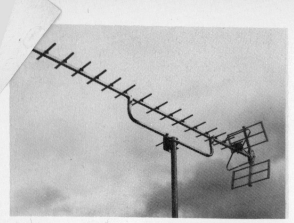

A Group C standard in-line Yagi (QR18, Wolsey Electronics)

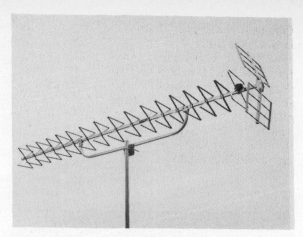

The HG36 high gain multiple director system (Wolsey Electronics)

The PBM18, on 18-element array featuring a modified slot dipole structure (Jaybeam Ltd)

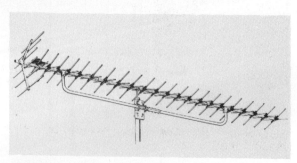

Available in both grouped and wideband, the XG21 multiple director high gain UHF array used full wave director units (Antiference Ltd)

A multiple director array, the JBX10 (Jaybeam Ltd)

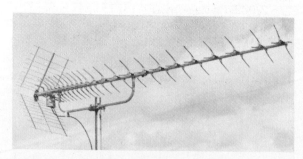

A West Germany wideband UHF array, the Fuba XC391 (imported by Audio Workshops)

in the United Kingdom so that in any one service area the transmissions originate from one transmitter site and that these channels are restricted into a channel grouping — this is in the interests of minimising interference with adjacent service areas and for the optimum reception quality on the home receiver.

The channel grouping currently employed is:

Group A	ch. 21–34
Group B	ch. 39–53
Group C/D	ch. 48–68
Group E	ch. 39–68
Group W	ch. 21–68

Continental European designs tend to be divided into a basic Band 4 — ch. 21—37; Band 5 — ch. 39—68, and further sub-divisions. One interesting feature is that a wide band UHF multiple director design is usually provided covering the whole of Bands 4 and 5. British arrays of the multiple director range have tended to be restricted into the various channel groupings as detailed above but at the time of writing several manufacturers have now introduced wide band versions.

A wideband UHF Log Periodic aerial type LBM2 (Jaybeam Ltd)

The wide band UHF aerial situation remained static for some years in the UK with generally the Log Periodic system being the only array with coverage in both bands. This array differs from the Yagi in that all elements are active and although the gain is somewhat lower than an equivalent Yagi with the same number of elements, it produces an extremely clean polar diagram with very low side lobe radiation patterns. The bandwidth and gain figures maintain a relatively level response throughout its designed frequency limits. The first 'breakthrough' in higher gain wide band UHF systems was the introduction of a stacked bowtie array, an aerial that had been very popular in the United States for many years. The 4 bay stacked bowtie typically has a gain of 11—13 dB over the whole UHF band, this in a shallow curve with the peak of 13 dB between ch. 50—ch.60. This type of array has a reduced performance out of band and will give satisfactory results into the 435—440 MHz amateur band, making it an ideal system for both TV-DXing and amateur TV (ATV) reception.

When equipped with a matching wide band UHF amplifier the long distance enthusiast had the best compromise for his activities. Antiference have also introduced wide banded versions for the whole UHF band in their 'XG' range and possessing a very high gain, characteristic of the multiple director system, and several imported ' X ' director aerials are now available on the UK market.

The typical multiple full wave X director system in the '91 element' versions has a gain peak of 16—17 dB (ref ½ wave dipole) in a wideband ch. 21—68 coverage aerial and with a low gain of 10—11 dB over the ch. 21—ch. 24 part of its coverage. The rising gain characteristic is typical of the long multiple director Yagi. Beamwidth also changes with increasing frequency and rising gain, sharpening to perhaps 23° at 3 dB points at the top end of its coverage in Group C/D and with a much wider 40° over the ch. 21 bottom end of its coverage.

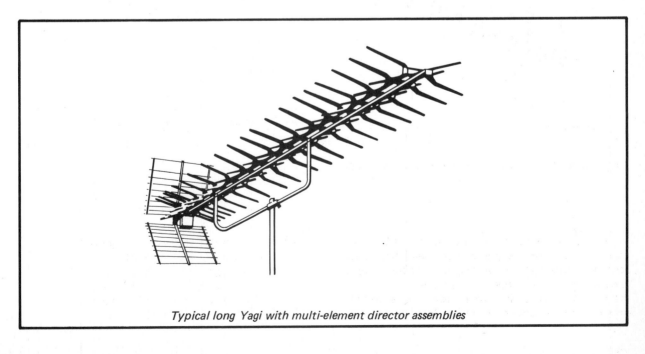

Typical long Yagi with multi-element director assemblies

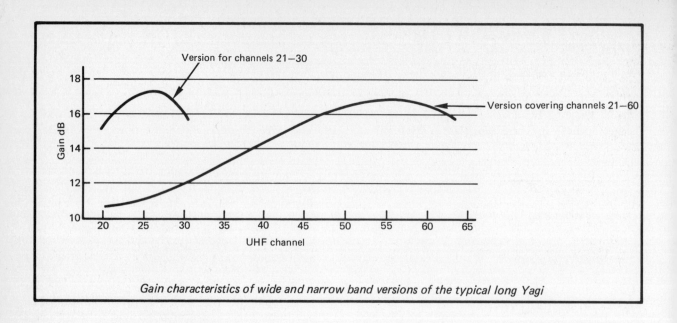

Gain characteristics of wide and narrow band versions of the typical long Yagi

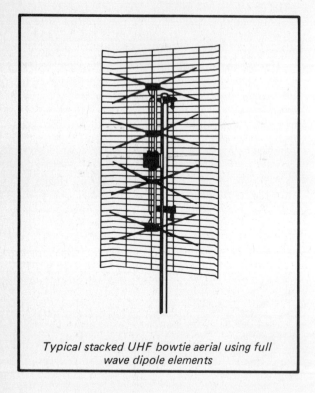

Typical stacked UHF bowtie aerial using full wave dipole elements

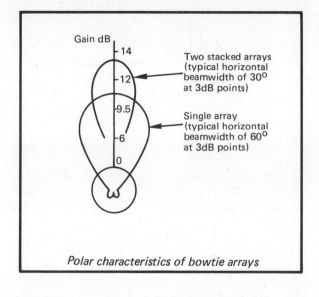

Polar characteristics of bowtie arrays

The stacked bowtie in its single version features a 3 dB beamwidth at typically 60° through much of its UHF bandpass, though this can be dramatically reduced by stacking a second similar array in side by side formation — reducing the 3 dB beamwidth to the 35° figure and increasing the gain by almost 3 dB; giving a 13–15 dB gain over the whole UHF band which compares favourably with the long multiple director Yagi. Low loss wideband stripline combining filters are available for either twin or quad stacked

formations. The twin stacked bowtie system enjoys an increasing popularity for TV-DXing due to its level characteristics, relatively small size, minimal wind resistance and competitive price structure when compared with a good quality long X Yagi aerial.

Above its designed high frequency cut-off, a long Yagi becomes completely non-directional due to the reflector action from the directors. Certain imported X Yagis are designed to a high frequency roll-off of ch. 60 or ch. 62 which results in a considerable fall in aerial performance over the top channels in UK Group C/D.

An entrant to the wideband UHF field that unfortunately enjoyed a brief commercial life was the Short Backfire. This aerial was based upon a Czechoslovakian design (although there are claims that the design originated in the U.S.A.) and departs

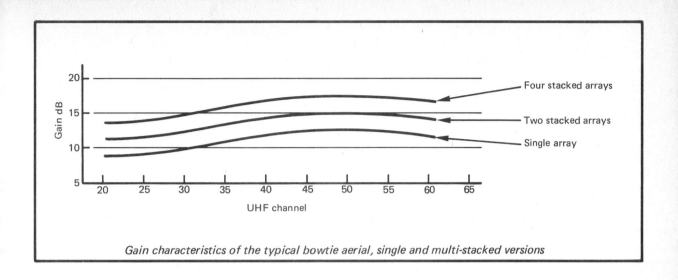

Gain characteristics of the typical bowtie aerial, single and multi-stacked versions

from the conventional UHF array in common use. The array featured a good bandwidth performance particulary when a 7-element director extension was fitted and a stacked array exhibited phenomenally deep nulls in its polar diagram allowing unwanted

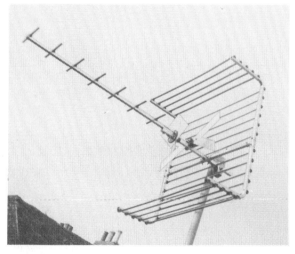

An unusual wideband UHF array, the Short Backfire (formally Telerection Ltd)

signals to be 'lost' and with 'on beam' gains of 15 dB in Group A to 19 dB at the high frequency end of Group C/D. A large reflector screen some 24 inches square in conjunction with a smaller reflector form a cavity resonator, signal pickup is with the shallow ' X ' dipole between the two reflectors. The gain rises from a low of 12 dB at the low frequency end to above 16 dB at the high frequency end of the UHF band. An aerial that is used extensively for deep fringe working in the United States is the Dish Reflector. A high gain array it usually features a single or stacked bowtie facing in the dish, the dish

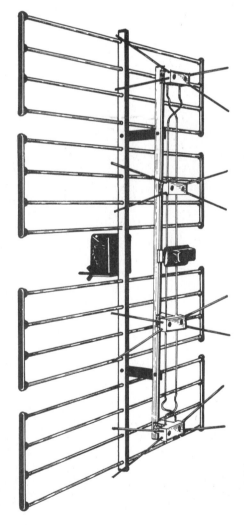

The Wolsey "Colour King" wideband UHF array using stacked dipole assemblies (Wolsey Electronics)

itself often measuring some 7 foot high and 5 foot wide.

The gain of an aerial can be increased by combining its signal output with another similar aerial mounted in close but calculated proximity. When such aerials are combined (or stacked) an alteration also occurs to the polar diagram. For vertically polarised arrays stacked side-by-side the forward pickup lobe is considerably sharpened. Horizontal arrays may be stacked side-by-side or above each other. Sideways stacking sharpens the forward pickup lobe, but stacking vertically above each other only marginally narrows the forward pickup lobe, but it does reduce the vertical acceptance angle. As signals can at times be received via Meteor Scatter in Band 3, sideways stacking is to be preferred, to exploit the wider vertical acceptance angle.

Stripline combiners are now available that permit twin or quad stacking at wide band UHF and still retain full bandwidth operation with very low insertion loss. There are also available wideband ferrite cored aerial combiners for VHF/UHF use but these unfortunately exhibit slight insertion losses, typically 0.5 dB and 1 dB VHF and UHF respectively. Group UHF arrays can be stacked to obtain an extra 3 dB power gain over the bandwidth and the spacing between the arrays can provide a useful method of adjusting the polar diagram to give nulls in directions that may be introducing interference into the receiving system.

As a general receiving standard, for long distance television reception, aerials should be mounted horizontally. With the exception of the United Kingdom and some countries in Europe, most high powered transmitters use horizontal polarisation. Due to the changing polarisation often noted with Sporadic E signals, an array can be mounted to advantage vertically in areas where strong local horizontally polarised transmissions occur, or vice versa if the local transmitter uses vertical polarisation. This will result in a considerable reduction of local transmitter interference.

The use of circular polarisation rather than a single plane polarisation in television transmission is likely to become widespread through North America and elsewhere during the next few years at UHF. Circular polarisation (CP) has advantages in built up areas with ghost reduction and with improving the results from indoor aerials of random polarisation. Fringe area performance however may deteriorate if the transmitter power or its aerial gain is not increased. CP signals are compatible with any plane polarised array, the array responding equally well mounted in either the vertical or horizontal plane provided it is perpendicular to the propagation path. The CP signal is transmitted with a clockwise rotating field (right hand – RH) or an anti-clockwise rotating field (left hand – LH) – this rotation when viewed from the aerial looking towards the propagation direction. Optimum signal output from a CP

array occurs when both transmitting and receiving arrays are of the same rotational sense, minimal performance is obtained when using CP arrays of opposite rotational sense.

Gaining popularity are 'active aerials'. These are basically a compressed array featuring inductive loading within specially designed containers resulting in reduced dimensions for Band 1 and 2 arrays. Dimensions of these containers are such that Band 3 and UHF arrays can be made to their normal resonant lengths. Typical sizes for these arrays are in the order of 80–100 cms for VHF types and reducing to perhaps 40 cms for UHF only systems, and appearance is usually that of a flat horizontal disc or fluted dome. By their very name 'active aerials' contain integral amplification stages to give both matching and gain, versions without integral amplifiers have outputs ranging to –6 dB in Band 1 and decreasing to –2 dB at UHF. Typical outputs from such compressed 'active aerials' are +15–20 dB at VHF, +25–30 dB at UHF, related to a ½ wave dipole.

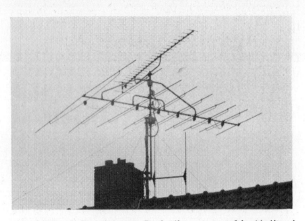

A wideband Band 1 Log Periodic on a roof in Holland

Where possible the aerials should be mounted in the open and away from obstructions. The type and height of a mast supporting an aerial will depend largely upon local conditions, hills, trees and neighbouring terrain, the attitude of planning authorities and personal economics. Sporadic E signals can be well received on low aerials although it is preferable to lift such an array to a minimum of 25 feet. Tropospheric reception necessitates a greater degree of aerial selection and positioning with the use of high gain arrays at the maximum height possible. For both Sporadic E and Tropospheric reception, a slight upward tilt of 5–10° to the receiving aerial is often beneficial.

For multi-element arrays, arrangements should be made to rotate the system either by mechanical or electrical means; rotor units are now available from various aerial suppliers. Precautions should be taken to allow sufficient cable slackness at points between moving and fixed parts of the mast, in order to avoid cable stress and damage.

The maximum space possible should be allowed between separate aerials on the same mast in the interests of avoiding signal absorption and other undesirable effects. When mounting aerials upon a mast care should be taken to observe wind loading and other stresses that may occur should too many large arrays be fitted.

Once the aerial has extracted a weak signal from the ether it passes it to the receiver through the feeder cable. This will be of two types: coaxial cable or ribbon feeder. It is essential that the feeder has very low loss figures. Coaxial cable has an inner conductor, which with low loss cable is a single solid conductor, the surrounding dielectric consisting of cellular polythene or airspaced ribbon polythene. Ribbon feeder varies somewhat, often with a hollow tube construction, at times foam filled. Greater care has to be taken when fitting ribbon feeder to a mast, it being held away from the actual metalwork to avoid losses. Certain types of ribbon feeder have a very low signal loss when dry, unfortunately the losses tend to rise when the ribbon becomes wet. The signal loss within a feeder system will also rise with an increase in frequency. Whichever type of feeder is used, wise policy will dictate that the best quality is fitted. The table shows characteristics of four different types of coaxial cable often used for television aerial feeder. The stranded inner conductor coaxial cable has by far the greatest signal loss and should be avoided at all frequencies when used in weak signal work.

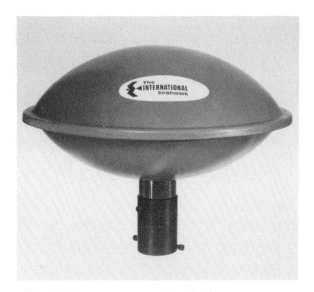

A wideband VHF/UHF 'active aerial' intended for marine use. Some 20'' in diameter, it features an integral wideband amplifier of some 27 dB gain, noise 5.5 dB and coverage of 40–860 MHz (Aeranamics Electronics Ltd, Peterhead)

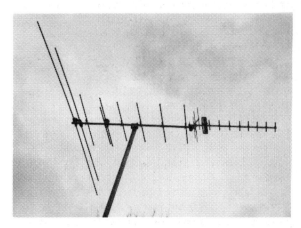

A wideband Band 1 dipole; a wideband Band 3 6-element aerial headed by a commercial wideband 10-element UHF Yagi (Antiference), giving wideband TV coverage on a single boom

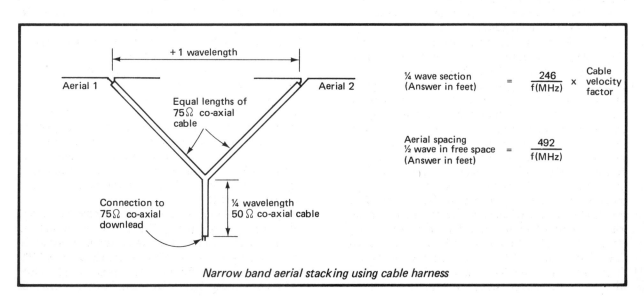

Narrow band aerial stacking using cable harness

$$\text{¼ wave section (Answer in feet)} = \frac{246}{f(MHz)} \times \text{Cable velocity factor}$$

$$\text{Aerial spacing ½ wave in free space (Answer in feet)} = \frac{492}{f(MHz)}$$

Type	Inner conductor		Polythene dielectric	Cable diameter (mm)	Capacitance (pf/metre)	Nominal attenuation dB/100 metres				
	No. of wires	Wire dia. (mm)				50 MHz	100 MHz	200 MHz	650 MHz	850 MHz
4202	7	0.25	Cellular	5.10	56	7.2	10.2	14.5	17.2	31.4
4203	1	1.12	Cellular	7.25	56	5.2	7.4	10.4	19.6	27.8
4205	1	1.25	Aeraxial	7.15	57	4.6	6.5	9.2	17.2	19.9
4209	1	1.40	Aeraxial	8.00	56	4.0	5.7	8.0	14.8	17.0
2010	2x7	0.28	PE				4.5	7.0	14.0 @ 600 MHz	17.0 @ 800 MHz

AERIALITE COAXIAL CABLE — types 4202, 4203, 4205, 4209

STOLLE 300 OHM RIBBON CABLE — type 2010

AERIAL TERMINOLOGY

Gain

This denotes the efficiency of a receiving array in terms of an improvement in signal output as compared (usually) with a half wave dipole. The power gain of an aerial is measured in decibels (dB). An improvement in gain of 3 dB denotes a doubling in signal output and usually the actual physical dimension of a receiving array is doubled to obtain the 3 dB gain.

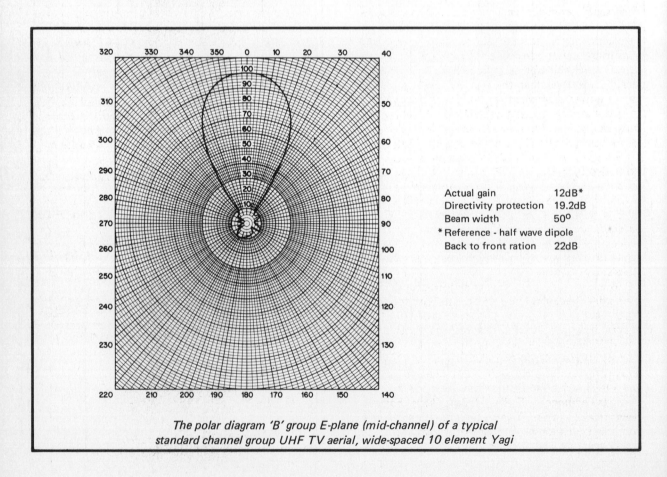

Actual gain   12dB*
Directivity protection   19.2dB
Beam width   50°
* Reference - half wave dipole
Back to front ration   22dB

The polar diagram 'B' group E-plane (mid-channel) of a typical standard channel group UHF TV aerial, wide-spaced 10 element Yagi

Decibel

A logarithmic unit of measurement denoting signal levels, gain and loss. Decibel ratio charts are given in many radio reference books.

Signal voltage

This is normally expressed in microvolts or millivolts (μV and mV). One mV = 100 μV. Often expressed in dBmV or dBμV: e.g. 0 dBmV = 1 mV.

Front to Back Ratio

This ratio is measured in dB and indicates the efficiency in receiving the required forward approaching signal compared with the efficiency in rejecting the unwanted signal arriving over the rear (reflector) end of the aerial.

Beamwidth/Acceptance Angle

This is an indication of the directional ability of a receiving aerial. The beamwidth is usually measured between the half power (3 dB) points on the required forward approaching signal.

Voltage Standing Wave Ratio (VSWR)

The ratio of the maximum voltage set up along a line and compared to the minimum voltage and is an index of the matching/mismatching properties of a line, the aerial and terminating receiver. A well designed commercial array will often present a VSWR of 1.5/1 or better whereas a home constructed Band 1 may display a VSWR of 2/1 or worse, depending on the efficiency of design and bandwidth covered.

Polar Diagram

The polar diagram of an array is the response pattern as the array is rotated through 360° whilst receiving a signal from a specific direction. If the signal output from the array is plotted on a 360° graph, its measurements corresponding to the aerial position a drawing is obtained showing the characteristics of the array such as beamwidth, front/back and the side lobe pattern.

AERIAL AMPLIFIERS

The signal strengths encountered with very weak distant television transmitters are such that they often lie below that of the receiver's threshold sensitivity and are unusable. At such times the use of an aerial amplifier is invaluable to lift the weak signal to a level that the receiver can accept and produce a recognisable image.

The transistor aerial amplifier has now come into universal use with a low noise performance superior to its valve counterpart. The low input impedance allows good matching (and a consequent minimum noise figure) from a 75 ohm aerial feeder, and assists with the design of amplifiers requiring a wide bandwidth. With the use of wide band aerials (which have a gain inversely proportional to bandwidth), an aerial amplifier of similar coverage allows for an efficient receiving system. As a general rule noise tends to increase with frequency for both valve and transistor circuits.

To maintain the lowest noise performance possible on a wide band amplifier, which will tend to have a higher noise for a given transistor than that of a narrow band amplifier, the use of UHF devices at both UHF and VHF is advised.

This revised edition includes new aerial amplifier designs for use at VHF and UHF using later devices and with lower noise figures than those shown in the previous editions. Earlier designs have however been retained since these offer variations to the later circuits and give an alternative approach for circuit modifications, incorporating ideas from earlier

designs with devices from more recent times. The BF180, for example, commonly featured in following pages, provides an inexpensive device for experimentation, though its noise figure at UHF is unacceptable for serious weak signal work.

Several circuit designs have been given using the BF180 in use at VHF and UHF with gains in a wide band circuit of 16 dB at Band 1, 14 dB at Band 3, 12 dB at Band 4 falling to 10 dB at Band 5. The expected noise figures will vary from 2 dB at Band 1

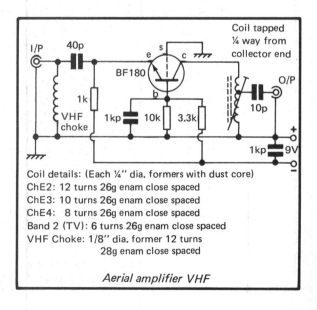

Aerial amplifier VHF

Coil details: (Each ¼" dia. formers with dust core)
ChE2: 12 turns 26g enam close spaced
ChE3: 10 turns 26g enam close spaced
ChE4: 8 turns 26g enam close spaced
Band 2 (TV): 6 turns 26g enam close spaced
VHF Choke: 1/8" dia. former 12 turns
28g enam close spaced

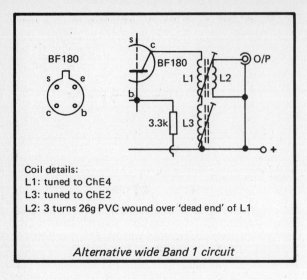

Coil details:
L1: tuned to ChE4
L3: tuned to ChE2
L2: 3 turns 26g PVC wound over 'dead end' of L1

Alternative wide Band 1 circuit

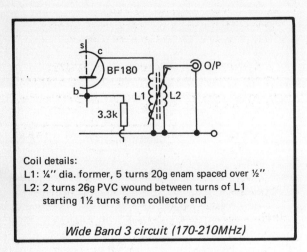

Coil details:
L1: ¼" dia. former, 5 turns 20g enam spaced over ½"
L2: 2 turns 26g PVC wound between turns of L1
   starting 1½ turns from collector end

Wide Band 3 circuit (170-210MHz)

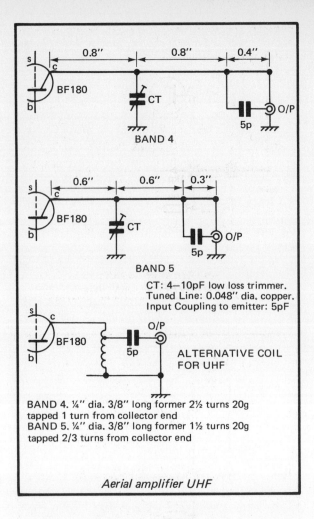

BAND 4

BAND 5

CT: 4—10pF low loss trimmer.
Tuned Line: 0.048" dia. copper.
Input Coupling to emitter: 5pF

ALTERNATIVE COIL
FOR UHF

BAND 4. ¼" dia. 3/8" long former 2½ turns 20g
tapped 1 turn from collector end
BAND 5. ¼" dia. 3/8" long former 1½ turns 20g
tapped 2/3 turns from collector end

Aerial amplifier UHF

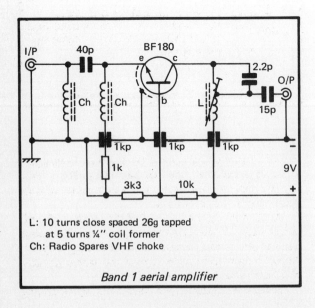

L: 10 turns close spaced 26g tapped
   at 5 turns ¼" coil former
Ch: Radio Spares VHF choke

Band 1 aerial amplifier

to 6 dB at Band 5. As a general rule stages may be cascaded to give increased gain but care must be taken in the interests of stability and a level gain/bandwidth performance.

Alternative circuits are given for later production transistor types BF272, BF362 and a skeleton circuit for the BF479. This latter circuit may be used at either VHF or UHF in wide or narrow band mode. The gain to be expected in Band 1 for a single stage will approach 20dB and with a noise figure of under 3dB.

A very successful low noise UHF amplifier can be made utilising the SGS BF679 and a single stage amplifier operating in a narrow band mode can realise 24 dB gain with a noise figure of under 2 dB.

An interesting circuit that can be tuned throughout Band 1 uses 2 Field Effect transistors type 2N3823E. Tuning is carried out with the 2 varicap diodes type BA110 although other diodes could be used if available. The advantage with using an FET circuit is the freedom from cross modulation and inter modulation which can easily occur with bipolar transitors if overloading due to excessive signal input takes place. The gain of the twin stage FET aerial amplifier should be in excess of 20 dB and with a

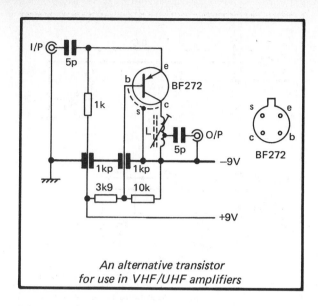

*An alternative transistor
for use in VHF/UHF amplifiers*

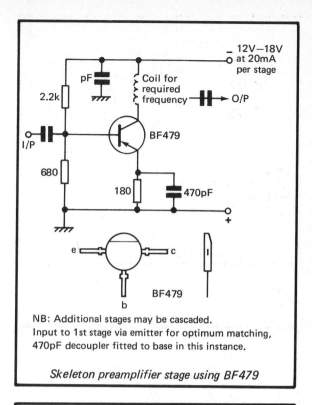

NB: Additional stages may be cascaded.
Input to 1st stage via emitter for optimum matching,
470pF decoupler fitted to base in this instance.

Skeleton preamplifier stage using BF479

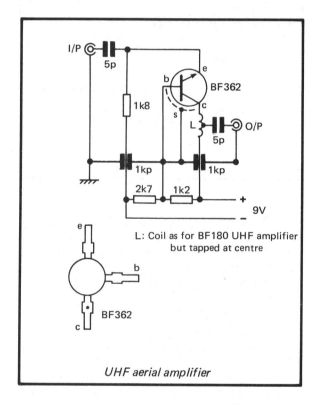

L: Coil as for BF180 UHF amplifier
but tapped at centre

UHF aerial amplifier

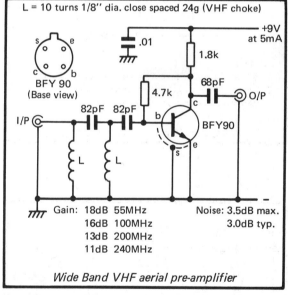

Wide Band VHF aerial pre-amplifier

very low noise figure.

There has been a tendency in recent years for manufacturers to market wide band amplifiers covering the total spectrum used by current television transmissions namely 40–860 MHz. Such amplifiers are now available having voltage gains of 25 dB with noise figures of under 2 dB. Mullard Limited have introduced a range of hybrid VHF/UHF amplifiers having various gains and noise figures, an example being the OM335 featuring a gain of 27 dB with

a noise figure of 5.5 dB. The amplifier is encapsulated in a ceramic type coating, measuring 1 inch by ½ inch and contains all components, merely requiring 24 volts at 35 mA.

A 12 volt version, type OM361, with a 28 dB gain, noise 6 dB is available with an alternative pin out structure as detailed in the following diagram. Signal output handling is higher and where possible this later version should be used.

Several enthusiasts have succeeded in modifying

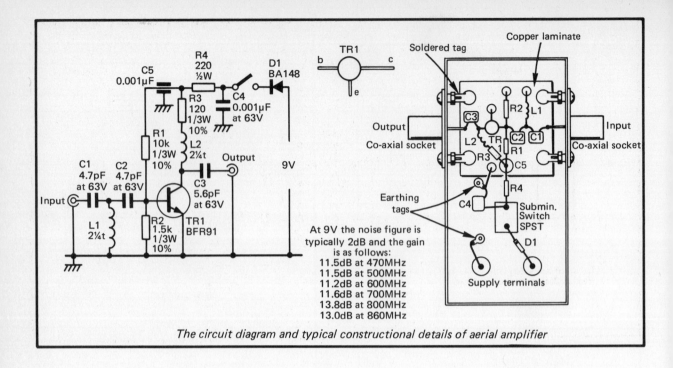

At 9V the noise figure is typically 2dB and the gain is as follows:
11.5dB at 470MHz
11.5dB at 500MHz
11.2dB at 600MHz
11.6dB at 700MHz
13.8dB at 800MHz
13.0dB at 860MHz

The circuit diagram and typical constructional details of aerial amplifier

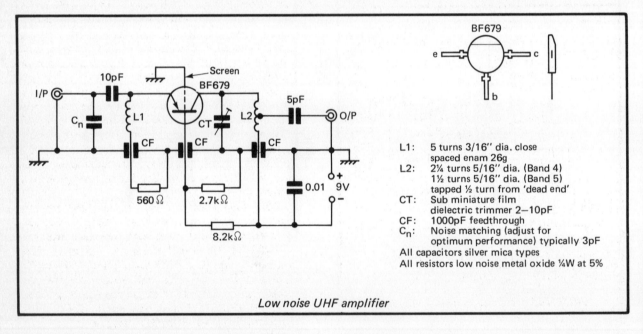

L1: 5 turns 3/16" dia. close spaced enam 26g
L2: 2¼ turns 5/16" dia. (Band 4) 1½ turns 5/16" dia. (Band 5) tapped ½ turn from 'dead end'
CT: Sub miniature film dielectric trimmer 2—10pF
CF: 1000pF feedthrough
Cn: Noise matching (adjust for optimum performance) typically 3pF
All capacitors silver mica types
All resistors low noise metal oxide ¼W at 5%

Low noise UHF amplifier

commercial TV tuners into high performance, high gain narrow band amplifiers. Valve tuners have been modified simply by removal of +HT voltage to the oscillator stage and RF output being taken from the anode of the mixer stage. Transistor UHF tuners have similarly been modified with the removal of the appropriate oscillator capacitor and coupling thereto, output being taken from the mixer collector. It has been possible to modify a varicap tuner in this way and fit the unit to the aerial itself, tuning being carried out adjacent to the receiver.

Masthead amplifiers are commercially available intended for aerial head mounting, thus amplifying the weak signal before any attenuation occurs in the feeder.

Typical masthead amplifier noise figures available for domestic units at UHF can now be expected at 2 dB or lower and use of the lowest noise amplifier possible at masthead is essential to optimise overall receive system noise performance. If an excessive cable run is used prior to amplification the noise degradation will increase since the dB loss of the intervening cable will add to the noise figure. It is

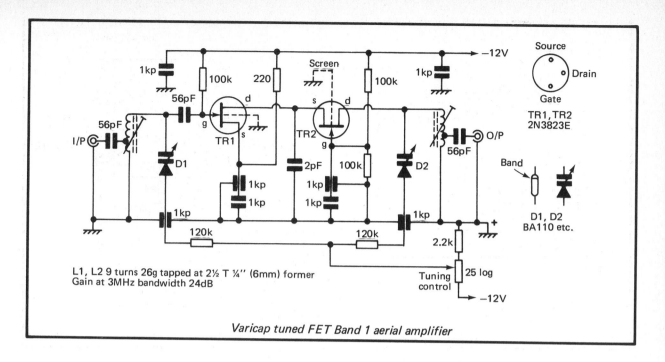

Varicap tuned FET Band 1 aerial amplifier

L1, L2 9 turns 26g tapped at 2½ T ¼″ (6mm) former
Gain at 3MHz bandwidth 24dB

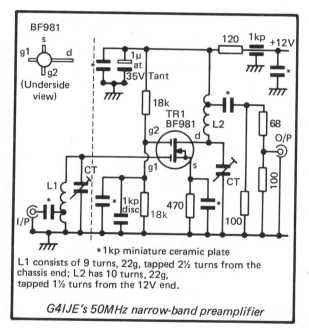

*1kp miniature ceramic plate

L1 consists of 9 turns, 22g, tapped 2½ turns from the
chassis end; L2 has 10 turns, 22g,
tapped 1½ turns from the 12V end.

G4IJE's 50MHz narrow-band preamplifier

usual) the RF stage is bipolar — which will lead to severe picture distortion, sound on vision/vision on sound and spreading of a 'local' signal across all immediate non-occupied channels in the local group and with a confusion of all 4 local channels superimposed on local channels. Moderation in gain within the local aerial grouping is therefore essential. If a MOSFET UHF tuner is in use then such cross modulation/overload effects are minimised. Unfortunately bipolar tuners which are more prone to overload generally exhibit lower noise figures than MOSFET types. Low level, low noise gain feeding a MOSFET tuner is perhaps the best compromise in current receiver technology.

Masthead power is fed to the head amplifier along the common feeder line. These are available in narrow or wide band units covering the total 40–900 MHz, each transmission group at UHF namely Groups A, B, C/D and W, total VHF of 40–250 MHz or the separate VHF bands. Typical gains range from 12 dB for a single stage unit in Group C/D, 30 dB for a 3 stage wide band UHF to 22 dB for a wide band 40–900 MHz 2 stage unit.

Higher performance units with medium gain and low noise at wide band UHF such as 15 dB gain, 1.6 dB noise are currently manufactured. VHF mastheads tend to feature higher noise levels, a Band 3 unit having 20 dB at 2.5 dB noise is typical. Band 1 head amplifiers are best avoided in the interests of minimising Citizens Band breakthrough of an harmonic nature (2 x 25 MHz = 54 MHz) and of course immediate neighbourhood radiation from cordless phones, 50 MHz amateurs and other unwanted problems. For Band 1 use a good wide band Band 1 array, low loss coaxial cable, appropriate filtering where necessary and then an indoor

therefore very important to use low gain with low noise amplifiers rather than high gain with high noise. Where possible a low gain low noise masthead unit should be fitted adjacent to the array with, if necessary, a second amplifier with higher signal handling characteristics later in the feeder when a long cable run is used. Receiving system noise performance is established within the first amplification stages and so careful selection of the masthead unit within the above guidelines will improve weak signal results. Excessive gain can lead to gross overloading of the UHF tuner's front end — particularly if (as is

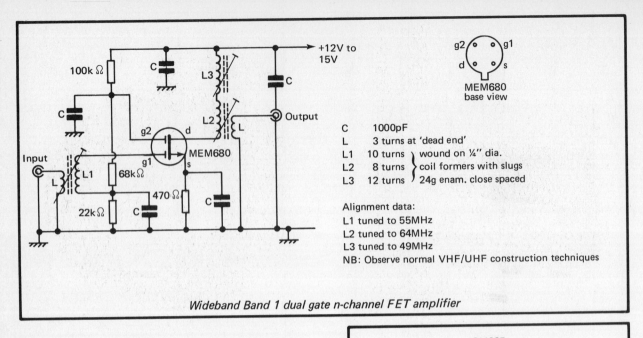

+12V to 15V

100kΩ
C
L3
C
C
Output
L2
L
g2 d
MEM680
g1 s
Input
L
L1
68kΩ
22kΩ
C
470Ω
C

g2 g1
d s
MEM680
base view

C   1000pF
L   3 turns at 'dead end'
L1   10 turns } wound on ¼" dia.
L2   8 turns } coil formers with slugs
L3   12 turns } 24g enam. close spaced

Alignment data:
L1 tuned to 55MHz
L2 tuned to 64MHz
L3 tuned to 49MHz
NB: Observe normal VHF/UHF construction techniques

Wideband Band 1 dual gate n-channel FET amplifier

amplifier (see section later on interference). A specialist aerial company should be consulted to establish the most suitable combination of amplifiers and filters for a given location and problem.

Amplifier (voltage) gain is always quoted in decibels (dBs) and often relates to a reference level which in TV distribution systems is 1 mV. Previously the dB gain discussion related to power gains and losses associated with aerials but with amplifier voltage gain the dB ratings differ somewhat. If an amplifier doubles a voltage then it has a gain of 6 dB, a gain of 4 times is 12 dB, and 18 dB gives 8 times amplification. Assuming we are relating these gains to the 1 mV reference the figure 6 dBmV = 2 mV (2 times 1 mV), 12 dBmV = 4 mV, 18 dBmV = 8 mV etc. The noise figure indicates the extra noise (snow on vision, hiss on sound) that the amplifier itself adds when amplifying the signal. Obviously we need to amplify the weak signal but add the minimum amount of noise. Cross modulation presents itself as buzzing, excessive contrast and the presence of other local channels onto an empty channel or by the appearance of several local signals on a single local channel. The cause is an excessive signal input into the amplifier stage to a degree that the transistor(s) are unable to present a linear characteristic. Most manufacturers will quote typical handling capacities which lowers if there are several local channels. One particular manufacturer quotes a wideband UHF amplifier as handling a single signal at 44.5 dBmV (167 mV) but with 4 local signals the handling drops to 39.5 dBmV (94 mV), the unit in question being a 2 stage amplifier. A single stage single group amplifier is quoted as 28 dBmV (25 mV) for a single signal falling to 23 dBmV (14 mV) in the presence of 4 signals. For distant signal work particularly on channels adjacent to strong local signals the import-

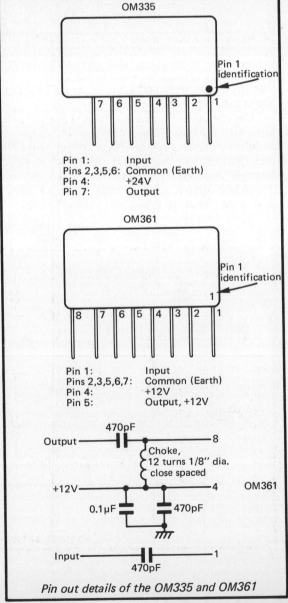

OM335

7 6 5 4 3 2 1

Pin 1 identification

Pin 1:   Input
Pins 2,3,5,6: Common (Earth)
Pin 4:   +24V
Pin 7:   Output

OM361

Pin 1 identification

8 7 6 5 4 3 2 1

Pin 1:   Input
Pins 2,3,5,6,7: Common (Earth)
Pin 4:   +12V
Pin 5:   Output, +12V

470pF
Output   8
Choke,
12 turns 1/8" dia.
close spaced
+12V   4   OM361
0.1µF   470pF

Input   1
470pF

Pin out details of the OM335 and OM361

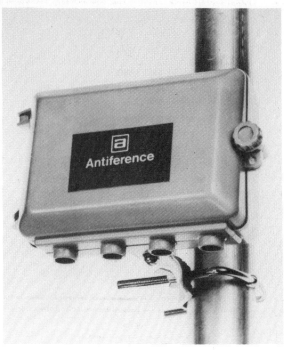

A typical masthead amplifier in its watertight case

A single stage 'group' masthead amplifier (Labgear Ltd)

ance of a low noise performance coupled with high signal handling capabilities will be obvious.

The advent of the Field Effect Transistor (FET) for VHF and UHF circuits should negate this problem — combining the advantages of valve operation with that of the bipolar transistor. A narrow band RCA MOSFET preamplifier is featured using the 40673 device. The amplifier has an extremely low noise figure and high gain characteristics. In operation the amplifier has given an extremely good account of itself at locations close to high powered transmitters and on closely adjacent frequencies where conventional bipolar devices would prove liable to excessive overload and cross modulation effects. For reasons of clarity protection diodes within the 40673 itself have been omitted from the circuit diagram.

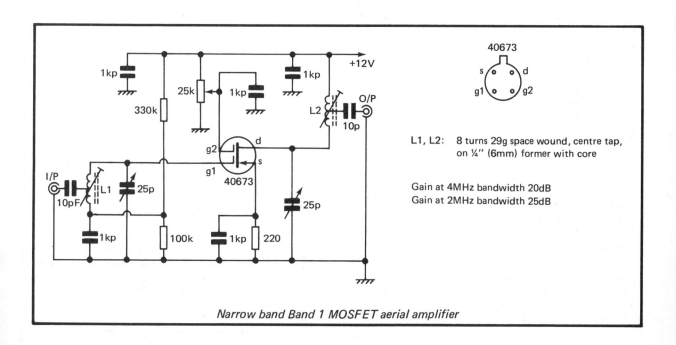

Narrow band Band 1 MOSFET aerial amplifier

L1, L2: 8 turns 29g space wound, centre tap, on ¼'' (6mm) former with core

Gain at 4MHz bandwidth 20dB
Gain at 2MHz bandwidth 25dB

A further interesting activity associated with long distance television is the photographing of the actual received image. Photography allows one to maintain a record of reception, comparisons of improvements over a period of time and facilitates identification of unknown signals. However greater skill is called for when photographing from the television screen but with some practice and experience excellent results can be obtained.

The use of a 35 mm camera is recommended, initially a cheap one should be obtained if venturing into this field for the first time. Such a camera is less expensive from an operating point of view, being able to take up to 36 full frame shots. It should be able to focus down to at least three feet and have either a shutter speed of under 1/25th or be capable of manual operation. The reason for the 1/25th speed is that each television picture is comprised of two interlaced fields, there being twenty-five complete pictures each second. If a shutter of 1/30th is used a complete scan of the picture is not achieved and the photograph will show the screen with some areas brighter than others. This effect can be quite marked on focal plane shutter cameras if a fast shutter speed is used. The Dutch test pattern clearly illustrates the shading that can occur with the use of a focal plane shutter. The shading pattern may disappear at shutter speeds greater than ¼ second. Experience has shown that the cheaper iris type shutter camera is ideal for TV-DX photography since it can work down to 1/15th second exposures with perfect results. Care must be taken to ensure accurate focusing and positioning of the camera when taking off-the-screen photographs. The normal minimum focus distance for the cheaper camera is 1 metre (3 feet) and with the use of a wide aperture the depth of focus will be relatively small calling for extreme accuracy in gaining optimum focus of the eventual print.

The basic exposure required for successful television screen shots is 1/15th at f.8 using a medium speed film such as Ilford FP4 (125 ASA), or 1/25th at f.5.6. A fast film can of course be used such as HP4 (400 ASA) but the aperture would need to be reduced to f.8 or f.11. Some experimentation may be necessary to determine the optimum settings and film type for a particular camera and surrounding room environment.

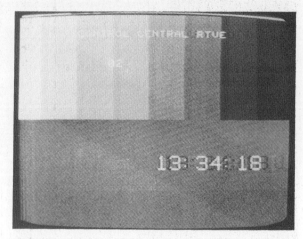

Another example of shading resulting from the use of a focal plane shutter camera

It is possible to use photography in assisting identification of weak signals using a method known as Time-Lapse Photography. The usual shutter speed as noted above is about 1/15th second and for moving subjects on the screen any longer exposure would result in blurring. Should however a stationary image — such as a test card, caption, etc. — be received but very weakly it is possible to remove much of the 'snow' and leave a recognisable picture. Noise is of a random nature and by exposing the film for up to one second many complete picture frames will be added together, the noise will tend to cancel out and the picture information will become much clearer. Since the long exposure time will allow a considerable amount of light to fall on the film the aperture must be reduced by the same factor or a slower film be used. Ilford Pan F (50 ASA) is the most suitable film using an aperture of f.22 with a shutter speed of one second. Alternatively neutral density filters may be used — a filter with a 'filter factor' of ×2 will allow the above camera setting but on FP4 film (125 ASA). There is a tendency for blurring when exposing for periods of one second due to sync jitter and longer exposures will tend to exaggerate this effect and of course increase the chances of sync slip.

When using a camera at such short focal lengths

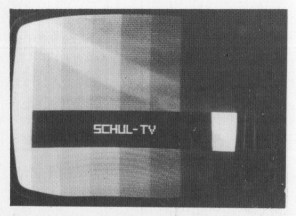

Shading effect caused by use of a focal plane shutter camera and too fast a shutter speed

Shot 1: exposure of 1/30th second at f5.6. This shows test card F with only main detail observable, the identification cannot be resolved. Considerable noise is present on the screen.

Shot 2: exposure of 2 seconds at f22 and using a x4 neutral density filter, Ilford FP4 film was used for this time lapse shot.

care should be taken to obtain the correct framing. Often the viewfinder is located above the lens assembly and appropriate adjustment should be made to prevent cutting off the top of the frame. A close-up lens can be used but this calls for extreme care with focusing distances. If it is possible to occupy the whole negative area with the television screen, the room in which the receiver is situated should be darkened, with no direct light falling onto the screen. However if the screen occupies part of the negative leaving a darker border, the room should be illuminated somewhat, allowing surrounding objects to be distinguished. The reason is that when printing, which is usually carried out with a machine, exposure takes into account the average brightness of the whole negative, tending to overexpose the subject in question. Actual enlargements can of course be made of the subject but these tend to be somewhat more expensive. When photographing from the screen the image should be set for normal contrast settings.

On no account should a flash attachment be used. If at all possible the camera should be mounted on a tripod or other solid object, especially if the shutter is operated manually. Should an unknown test card or caption appear, always resist the temptation of waiting for the signal to improve. It often doesn't! With the use of 35 mm film it is wise policy to take several shots of a test card and at a later time the best shot may be selected. Successful screen photography comes mainly from experience and it is suggested that some experimentation is initially carried out with various shutter and aperture settings in order to acquaint oneself with the techniques involved.

STATION IDENTIFICATION

Having equipped oneself for the reception of television signals over long distances, there then follows the problem of identifying the source of transmissions once the signal has been received. Fortunately within the European area a large number of countries have test transmissions during parts of the day, prior to programme commencement. The test cards used during trade tests usually carry some form of identification, but unfortunately such cards can be interspersed with other standard patterns — such as colour bars, line sawtooths, etc. When such common patterns are used the only way of identifying the source is to wait the appearance of the test card or if received during a Sporadic E opening, to note the general direction, the skip distance and source of other signals and then determine the transmitter/country being received by a method of elimination. The situation is further confused by a transmitter, within a network, originating its own pattern, whilst other network transmitters originate the test card. With the multiplicity of channel and frequency allocations in Europe careful observation of the channel being received will usually narrow the choice of possible transmitters. When most transmitters are carrying programme material the usual means of identification is between programmes when captions, clocks or announcers appear. At times, within Europe, a common programme is transmitted throughout certain countries via Eurovision and/or Intervision. The normal practice for such exchanges is to display a Eurovision/Intervision caption indicating the local network, followed with a similar caption indicating the programme originating network. Often the Intervision Network captions incorporate well known local views.

It is possible to identify a programme source from the sound channel if one is reasonably well versed in languages. Unfortunately many of the East European languages sound alike and as a general rule such identification is difficult for the person having little or no knowledge of such languages.

One method of station identification that has enjoyed a degree of success in recent years is by observation of the vertical interval test signal (VITS). If a strong signal from a local transmitter is tuned in and the field hold 'slipped' so that the picture rolls slowly downwards, a series of small lines, dots and other markings will be seen in the field pulse strip. Recently Oracle and Ceefax transmissions in the UK have also been included which will be identified by their continual moving action. The series of small lines and dots are test signals inserted during the field flyback interval in lines 19 and 20. Many European and other broadcasters now insert such test signals and it is possible to recognise individual transmission networks by their particular test signals. The test signals do of course change over a period but with a little practice it will be possible to identify a certain transmitter or country. The test signals are transmitted continually during normal 'test' transmissions and programme times. Some typical VITS patterns are illustrated which will give an idea as to their appearance.

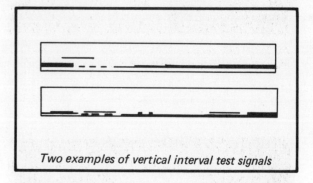

Two examples of vertical interval test signals

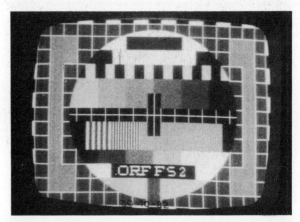

Philips PM5544 electronic test card — ORF (Austria) ch.E32 Tropospheric reception Holland (RMU)

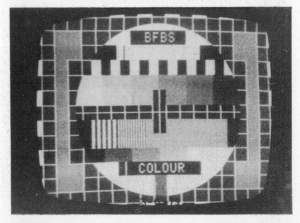

PM5544 card — West Germany — British Forces Broadcasting Service ch.E49 received Holland (RMU)

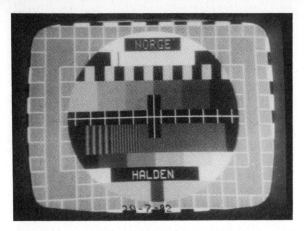

PM5544 test card — NRK (Norway ch.E11 received Holland (RMU) via Tropospheric propagation

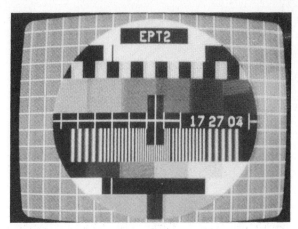

Variation on the 5544 theme, the PM5534 (clock insert) and less side panels — EPT (Greece) received Cyprus

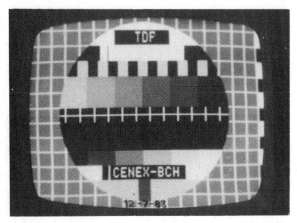

PM5544 variation — TDF (France)

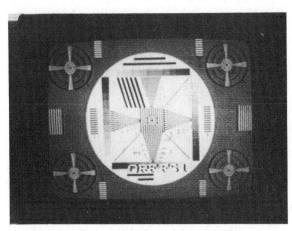

Telefunken (TO5) test card — ORF (Austria) ch.E2a received Aberdeen via Sporadic E

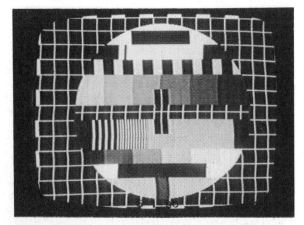

Further variation of PM5544 with dark background — TVP (Poland) ch.R1 via Sporadic E in Holland (RMU)

FUBK test card — RTP (Portugal) though this variation shows an Azores origination, seen on SATCOM 1/5 downlink during an outside broadcast

Variation to the Fubk, no circle — RTL (Luxembourg) ch.E21/27 in Holland (RMU)

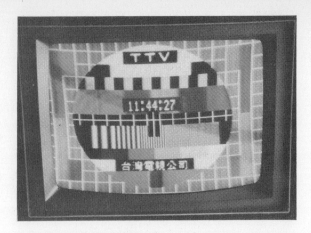

Variations on the PM5544 — Taiwan Television (note the focal plane shutter shading)

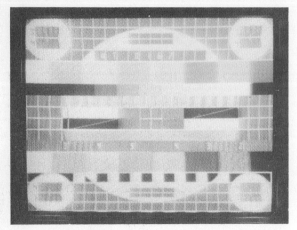

USSR 0167 type test card via the Gorizont spot beam at 3.675 GHz in Surbiton

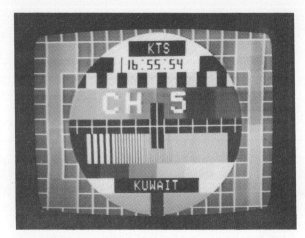

Kuwait Television test card, ch.5

North American test pattern — American Forces Network, West Germany (System M)

American Forces Network, Holland, ch.E70

In the Americas increasing use is made of offset patterning as a means for identifying an unknown transmitter. To improve co-channel interference rejection, certain transmitters are 'off-set' — that is to say: a transmitter will have its radiating frequency shifted somewhat from the nominal channel frequency by a certain amount, often 10–12 KHz. When two transmitters are received simultaneously on the same channel but with one off-set, a patterning will be apparent — caused by the beating of the two carriers. Having determined the amount by which the unknown transmitter is offset, reference to transmitter listings will narrow the field considerably, bearing in mind such factors as the general direction of reception, skip distance, etc.

A representative selection of test cards is shown mainly to illustrate the great variety and types now in use throughout the world. The whole subject of test cards has been covered in the publication *Guide to World-Wide Television Test Cards* by Keith Hamer and Garry Smith, and published by HS Publications, 17 Collingham Gardens, Derby, DE3 4FS, England, or *TV-Bildkatalog* by Norbert Kaiser distributed in the U.K. by Aerial Techniques whose address is shown on page 84.

For transmitter identification within the European area the enthusiast is recommended to subscribe to the EBU's massive *List of Television Stations*, an annual publication with six bi-monthly supplements. The supplements advise both opening and closing of transmitters and of changes in technical characteristics. The *List of Television Stations* is published on September 1st of each year and available from European Broadcasting Union (EBU), Centre Technique, 32 Avenue Albert Lancaster, 1180 Bruxelles, Belgium. Return postage should be included with any query.

INTERFERENCE

With television transmitters operational in most areas, often at high signal strengths, some interference must be expected on frequencies adjacent to occupied channels. The degree to which such interference occurs will depend upon the strength of the signal arriving at the receiver from the aerial and the performance of the various sections within the receiver itself. The question of IF strip selectivity has already been discussed and where possible the maximum protection against adjacent channel interference should be incorporated. This will ensure a constant standard of selectivity irrespective of the channel in use.

The notch filter as detailed proved a great success when Band 1 BBC-TV was transmitting since it was capable of high attenuation with a very steep skirt response, allowing reception on closely adjacent frequencies. With a Band 1 future in the UK dominated by other transmission sources (e.g. 50 MHz radio amateurs, cordless phones, PMR, etc.) and also for the assistance of overseas readers the notch filter data has been retained.

There may be occasions when one particular transmitter causes problems and one method of reducing such interference to a low level is with the aerial notch filter. The circuit of such a filter for use within Band 1 is illustrated, the response is such to provide an attenuation in the order of 40 dB or greater at resonance and allowing signals some 250 KHz to pass with a low order of attenuation. A notch filter of this type is particularly invaluable when used in the European area, where, due to the multiplicity of channel allocations, certain signals may lie extremely close together, an example being the ch. B3 sound frequency at 53.25 MHz and the ch. 1A video frequency at 53.75 MHz. The adjustment of the notch filter is extremely critical, the tuning must therefore be adjusted very slowly so as not to pass the notch. When the notch has been found the variable resistor is adjusted to give a further increase of attenuation, there being one critical value for this adjustment. As excellent as

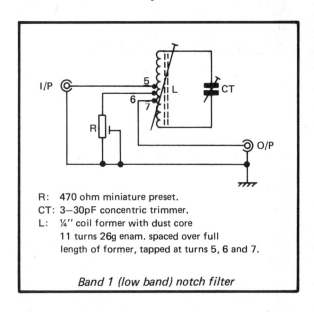

R: 470 ohm miniature preset.
CT: 3–30pF concentric trimmer.
L: ¼'' coil former with dust core
11 turns 26g enam. spaced over full
length of former, tapped at turns 5, 6 and 7.

Band 1 (low band) notch filter

this notch filter is, it cannot assist with co-channel signals; such as ch. E2 video and ch. B2 sound both at 48.25 MHz. In this case more experimentation may be necessary with a fixed aerial orientated to provide the minimum pickup of the strong unwanted signal. This method will give reasonable results with

Sporadic E propagation when signals are strong and with random polarisation.

The design of a double notch filter that features an insertion loss of only 1 dB with notch depths typically of 50 dB is shown and is intended for applications such as removal of a System A channel's sound and vision carrier frequencies. Experience has shown that attempts to notch out frequencies less than 1.5 MHz apart in an attempt to recover a middle frequency does tend to attenuate this latter frequency unduly.

An experimental Notch Filter for Band 3 is illustrated. This was used with great success by an enthusiast living some four miles from a very high powered transmitter in preventing severe cross-modulation and other spurious effects resulting from the strong overload of aerial amplifiers operating on adjacent channels. This design has been used with success in Band 1, but with the coil being modified somewhat. A Toroid core type T-50 10M1X is substituted and with ten turns of 20 g enamel wire tapped at five turns. Such Toroids have a higher Q than the standard core tuned coils due to the reduced number of turns needed.

This very simple Band 1 notch filter has a repeatable 26 dB notch depth and very low insertion loss off-notch as follows: +500 KHz = 10.2 dB; +1 MHz = 6 dB; +2 MHz = 2 dB; +3 MHz = 0.8 dB.

In areas adjacent to a high powered UHF transmitter, the latter's signals can often cross-modulate into other bands. This can easily be removed by a simple filter at the amplifier input. Such a filter can comprise a series inductance (say 2 turns, ¼ inch diameter) and capacitance (2–10 pf miniature low loss trimmer), the circuit being tuned to the mid-channel of the offending group. In severe cases an additional parallel tuned rejector circuit may be necessary in the aerial input (using similar components as before) in addition to the series tuned acceptor circuit. The former circuit is connected between the aerial input and chassis, the second between the aerial input and amplifier first stage.

Reversing the polarisation of the receiving aerial to that of the strong interfering signal can also give a considerable reduction in interference as discussed in the aerial section. Co-channel interference can also be reduced somewhat with the use of highly directional aerials and stacked arrays can be modified to remove unwanted signals from the rear. The

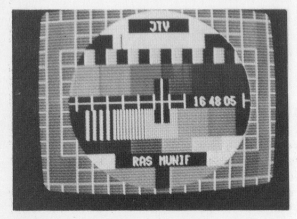

Co-channel interference on Jordan ch.E9 from Syrian transmitter, received in Cyprus

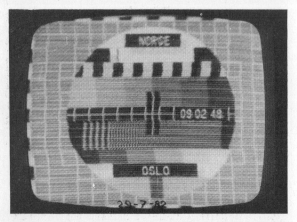

Co-channel interference during Tropospheric opening — NRK (Norway) ch.E6 in Holland (RMU)

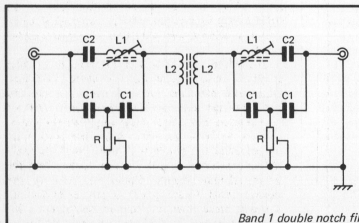

C1: 120pF
C2: 22pF
R: 470Ω min. preset
L1: 8 turns 26g ¼" (6mm) former
L2: 1/1 coupling transformer
    3 turns each 36g wound through ferrite bead
Notch depth 50dB, through loss 1dB

Band 1 double notch filter

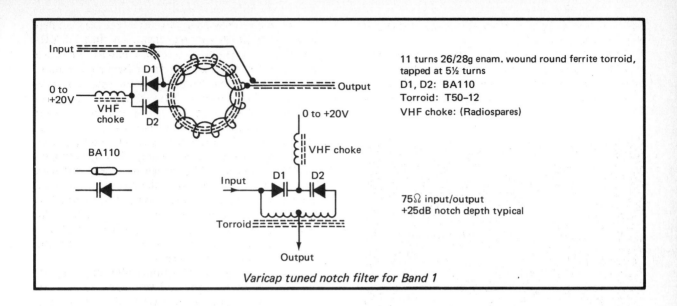

11 turns 26/28g enam. wound round ferrite torroid,
tapped at 5½ turns
D1, D2: BA110
Torroid: T50–12
VHF choke: (Radiospares)

75Ω input/output
+25dB notch depth typical

Varicap tuned notch filter for Band 1

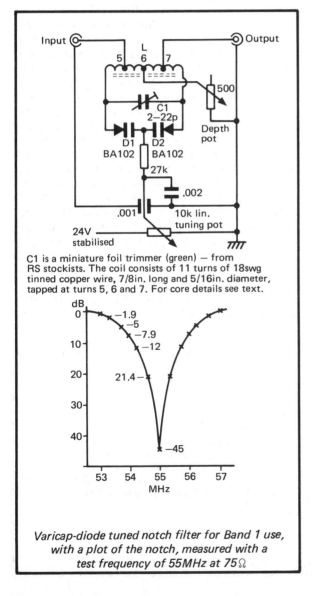

C1 is a miniature foil trimmer (green) — from
RS stockists. The coil consists of 11 turns of 18swg
tinned copper wire, 7/8in. long and 5/16in. diameter,
tapped at turns 5, 6 and 7. For core details see text.

*Varicap-diode tuned notch filter for Band 1 use,
with a plot of the notch, measured with a
test frequency of 55MHz at 75Ω*

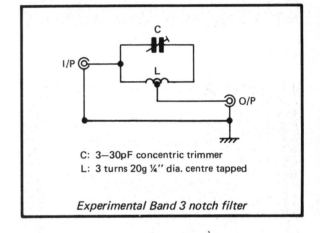

C: 3–30pF concentric trimmer
L: 3 turns 20g ¼'' dia. centre tapped

Experimental Band 3 notch filter

phasing harness of such a stacked array has an extra
¼ wave of feeder introduced into one section, and the
appropriate aerial is advanced ¼ wave in the forward
direction. Signals arriving from the forward direction
still combine at the junction of the phasing harness in
phase but signals arriving over the back of the aerial
are 180° out of phase at the junction (due to one
signal having to travel an extra ½ wavelength) resulting in a considerable reduction of the interfering
signal.

The advent of Citizens Band radio at 27 MHz
produced serious problems for many TV-DXers.
Either 2nd harmonic overload effects, or radiated
2nd harmonics were produced particularly by those
CB operators with illegal linear amplifiers (known as
'burners' to CB enthusiasts). A 27 MHz notch filter
will minimise the problem. These, which are available commercially or can be scaled down from the
designs already shown, should be fitted in the
receiver aerial feeder prior to any amplification.
A toroid break filter to minimise coaxial braid RF
currents adjacent to high power transmissions is

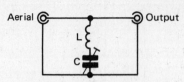

L: 5 turns ¼'' dia. 20g wire
C: 3—30pF miniature trimmer

ACCEPTOR CIRCUIT
for removing Band 2 FM radio breakthrough in other bands

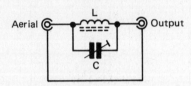

L: 4 turns 20g wire
wound on a ferrite core
C: 2—20pF miniature trimmer

REJECTOR CIRCUIT
for removing Band 3 breakthrough in Band 1
The trimmer is optional and should be used
if breakthrough is severe

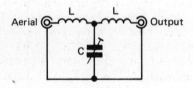

L: 2 turns ¼'' dia. 20g
air spaced over ¼''
C: 2—10pF miniature trimmer

ABSORPTION FILTER
to remove UHF breakthrough in Bands 1/3

NB: The solid inner conductor from low loss co-axial
cable is ideal for making the above coils.

*Filters to remove cross-band
interference breakthrough*

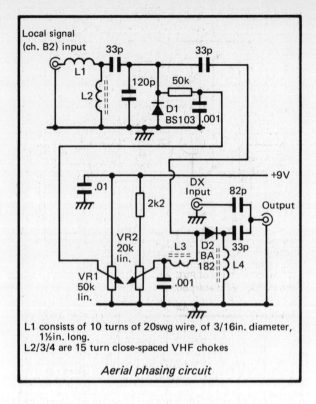

L1 consists of 10 turns of 20swg wire, of 3/16in. diameter,
1½in. long.
L2/3/4 are 15 turn close-spaced VHF chokes

Aerial phasing circuit

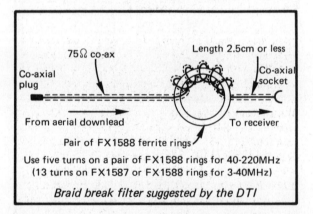

Use five turns on a pair of FX1588 rings for 40-220MHz
(13 turns on FX1587 or FX1588 rings for 3-40MHz)

Braid break filter suggested by the DTI

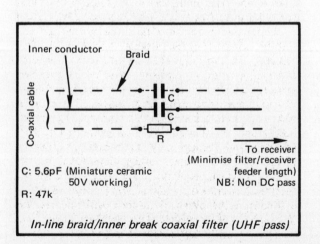

C: 5.6pF (Miniature ceramic
50V working)
R: 47k

NB: Non DC pass

In-line braid/inner break coaxial filter (UHF pass)

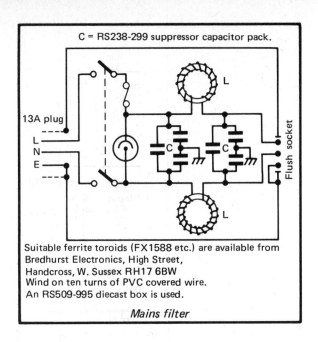

C = RS238-299 suppressor capacitor pack.

13A plug

L
N
E

L

L

C   C

Flush socket

Suitable ferrite toroids (FX1588 etc.) are available from
Bredhurst Electronics, High Street,
Handcross, W. Sussex RH17 6BW
Wind on ten turns of PVC covered wire.
An RS509-995 diecast box is used.

Mains filter

also shown. A simpler braid/inner break filter for UHF applications only is illustrated giving +30 dB stop at 27 MHz.

The Radio Services division of the Department of Trade and Industry have a considerable range of filters and if problems are experienced with breakthrough from a known source they can normally be called upon for advice.

It is advisable when a filter is used to remove an offending source of interference that the filter be inserted before any amplifier since the amplifier will undoubtedly exaggerate the problem.

ADDITIONAL CHANNELS

It is an interest of many TV-DXing enthusiasts to enhance home domestic TV entertainment by supplementing the locally available channels with additional programming from more distant (fringe) areas. British interest can occur for example from Welsh residents seeking UK Channel 4 as an alternative to S4C, by viewers wanting a second (commercial) ITV region, by coastal viewers along the South/East UK coast receiving French/Benelux TV services (with an appropriate standard TV) and Irish Republic viewers viewing UK transmissions. Overseas interests similarly are varied with signal interests such as South Spain/Gibraltar, Cyprus/ Greece and the multiplicity of Gulf/Middle East countries and states.

Requirements are obviously wide and varied and specific consultancy is essential to resolve a given receiving site. Information is needed such as required channel(s), locally received channels/frequencies, geographical location and terrain features, known and unknown sources of interference. This includes nearby transmitting sources, the receiving equipment, mast erection potential and local planning restraints (if any), and perhaps most significant the financial budget for the project under consideration. It follows that appropriate equipment to suit the received transmission standard will be purchased or is available in the event of interest with an overseas TV service. Weak signals are a problem but perhaps more of a difficulty in populated areas is that of

interference. Interference can arise from adjacent channel transmissions, from nearby radio transmitters (e.g. PMR, CB, amateur radio), medical radiation, usually at VHF, from electrical equipment such as motors and thermostats down to shaver socket isolation transformers! Other problems are motor ignition, home computers/VDUs, modern touch button and cordless telephones. The list is endless — any can play havoc with weak signals and each will require treatment at source or remedial action at the receiving site to minimise the interference levels.

Weak signals should be lifted with low noise amplifiers — if possible of limited bandwidth rather than the wide 40—860 MHz types that will exaggerate all problem sources throughout its designed bandwidth. Within a domestic pricing structure masthead amplifiers are available with bandwidths limited to the band (rather than an individual channel), e.g. Wideband Band 3 170—230 MHz, UHF either in UK groups or wide-band 470—860 MHz. Where possible filtering to reduce a problem should be fitted before amplification or if this is impossible a low gain low noise amplifier should be used initially to establish a low system noise and to overcome successive filter/ cable losses.

Many filters are available to remove a problem or to slope a specific band response — certain are made for external use in weatherproof housings. Just some of the types of RF filters are — Band pass, band stop, channel pass, group pass, channel stop, notch, double notch, high pass, low pass, braid break, diplex, triplex (VHF/VHF, VHF/UHF, UHF/UHF, VHF/UHF/UHF) and further variations such as 4 inputs with narrow bandpass inject. These are available for Band 1, 2, 3, UHF (wideband or group) use and generally of low insertion loss, with DC through pass on spurs. Input mains filters of capacitor/inductor construction can be used to reduce mains born interference though problems relating to mains equipment usually arrive as radiated interference pickup on the aerial system.

Interference from other transmitters can be minimised by correct selection of the aerial system if a single channel is required then an array minimising bandwidth should be used, both in the interests of maximising gain and reducing the beamwidth (i.e. making the optimum pickup pattern very narrow). If for example a ch.28 signal is required then a Group A array should be selected. Stacked aerials should be employed for increased gain and also for engineering polar diagram nulls and minimising side pickup. If mixing a distant UHF signal with a local (different channel) group, wideband combiners must be avoided — the local signals will come down the distant signal aerial and produce phase errors etc. when mixed with the local signal input via the local aerial. In this situation a UHF/UHF channel selective diplexer should be used. Most have, or can be modified for, a DC pass to a masthead amplifier. In-group mixing with a distant channel should include a channel pass filter in the 'distant' feed and a channel notch, tuned to the 'weak' channel, in the local feed.

Band 3 pickup is less severe for the various French/Benelux transmitters into the UK — though the future of Band 3 PMR in the UK coupled with the wide IF passbands of the domestic TV could mean severe intereference problems — again the use of a notch or stub filters appropriately tuned should negate the problem.

It will be obvious that in engineering additional channels problems may arise. In many situations a desired 'fringe' addition can easily be added, though care must be taken if the extra signal is diplexed into a common feeder. It is advisable to seek expert advice from a reputable aerial company when considering installation of more sophisticated dual station equipment if optimum results are to result.

Reception from Benelux/French stations which operate on systems B/G/L respectively at VHF/UHF will require a multi-standard TV receiver. RTE-Eire use System I but at both VHF and UHF, the easiest solution for the VHF coverage would be inclusion of a standard upconverter outputting at UHF into a standard System I receiver with preset tuning on the latter to correspond to the upconverter's output channels.

The above generalised information should give an idea as to the approach and problems of increasing

Inland 'pirate TV' operations can sometimes be received such as this ch.E28 transmission in the West London area

Pirate TV has been very active in Holland at UHF such as this Amsterdam station

The ch.E33 logo of ETB — Basque TV in North Spain

channel reception on an entertainment basis at a given home receiving site. Each situation has its own unique problems and should be resolved in conjunction with an expert aerial engineer. The BBC and IBA publish transmitter location guides which are available from their respective Engineering Information Departments free of charge; see appendix at end for addresses.

AMATEUR TELEVISION (ATV)

Amateur television (ATV) is a rather specialised form of amateur radio which allows a licensed amateur to transmit fast scan television pictures to broadcast standards within the 70 cms (435–440 MHz) band and the microwave 23/24 cms (1240–1325 MHz) band, using AM video at 70 cms and either AM or FM video modulation at 24 cms. The latter band is actually subdivided into segments since the spectrum is shared with other amateur users. The 24 cms band can be used for simplex operation (i.e. using a single frequency for contacts) or duplex via a repeater (i.e. transmitting a TV signal into a repeater at one frequency, it then re-radiates to a wider coverage area on another frequency simultaneously). Sound + vision transmissions to System I standards can be used at 24 cms. Vision signals may consist of test cards, computer graphics, colour/mono camera information of the operator, his equipment or a video tape of an interesting recording, transmissions usually being fairly short and identified with the call-sign of the transmitting operator. At times portable operation occurs where an amateur or group thereof will ascend a hill, or locate at a local show and transmit television from that site. From time to time ATV contests are held in which amateurs attempt to transmit to and receive from as many fellow enthusiasts as possible. TV-DXers can obviously participate in reception only when at such times activity is intense — particularly if a Tropospheric opening coincides. It is possible to receive amateur TV signals over many hundreds of miles at 70 cms though at 24 cms at the present time with far fewer enthusiasts active and the signal frequency itself being 'terrain conscious', signals may be limited in number. ATV operators are generally dedicated enthusiasts in a hobby that can involve a high degree of home construction in the transmission/receiving chain to a very impressive technical standard.

Reception of ATV at 70 cms involves an aerial; a Group A or stacked bowtie will work well, though filtering may be necessary in the direction of a high level Group A if head amplification is in use. As an alternative specific 70 cms aerials are available from amateur radio retail outlets (generally at 50 ohms impedance rather than the domestic norm of 75 ohms). Certain UHF tuners may tune down to 70 cms without modification. With the relative inexpensive 'surplus' UHF tuners available, a realignment of the tuned circuits to favour the 435–440 MHz spectrum only will result in a high performance unit. Dedicated ATV converters giving 435 MHz out at ch.36 can be purchased from amateur radio outlets or via mail order from specialised manufacturers.

The 23/24 cms band is a more specialised undertaking since we are in the realm of lower microwave and video transmission, maybe of either FM or AM video. The British Amateur Television Club (BATC) favours the establishment of FM at 24 cms and generally most amateurs transmit in this format. Frequency Modulated video uses wider bandwidths on transmit relating to deviation and the bandwidth of the input video itself. If for example a 5 MHz video bandwidth (no sound) is transmitted the effective bandwidth is approximately 19 MHz. Aerials are critical and expensive compared with the 70 cms equivalent; cable needs to be of very low loss characteristics even if a low noise GaAsfet head amplifier is used. Fortunately, as with 70 cms, specialised kits can be purchased for both head amplifier, downconverter and main receiver (UHF in, video/audio out at baseband) to simplify entry into 24 cms. In general terms the downconverter will accept the 24 cms input, with one (or more) stage of low noise amplification to produce an IF output at UHF for feeding to a receiver (using UHF as a second IF). Kits at present available opt for an FM video received format.

Despite the limitations imposed by local terrain, the increasing number of repeaters in regions where 24 cms ATV activity is high will allow an amateur with a very shielded location to 'access' a nearby repeater (which is normally sited on high ground) to retransmit his television picture to a very wide area.

ATV talkback/communication is at 144.750 MHz nominal ± 25 MHz (1 channel FM) and monitoring this frequency with a scanner or 2 metre receiver will give an indication of any local or semi-local activity. Contact with a local radio club may establish any local ATV operators who can be contacted — often a special transmission can be arranged for alignment of new equipment, tuner, converter, etc.

Interested ATV enthusiasts should join the BATC to exploit the hobby to the fullest — the address is in the conclusion at the end of this book. Finally if you actually receive an ATV transmission let the operator know — he will be pleased to hear from you!

Amateur TV station from Belgium at 435 MHz
(RMU)

Micro-computer generated station identification at
435 MHz

Amateur station in UK operating portable from
hilltop site near Shaftesbury, Dorset at 435 MHz

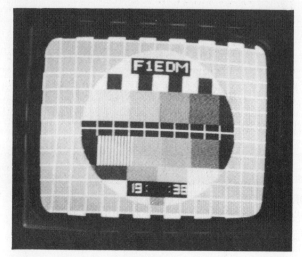

French amateur TV station at Le Havre received
in Southampton at 435 MHz

Pin Diode Variable Attenuator

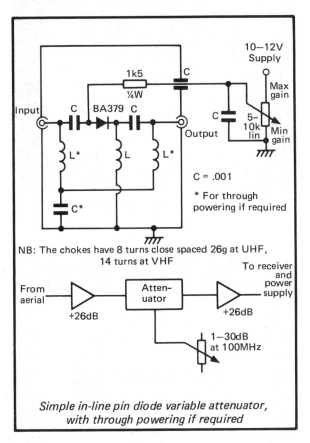

NB: The chokes have 8 turns close spaced 26g at UHF, 14 turns at VHF

C = .001

* For through powering if required

Simple in-line pin diode variable attenuator, with through powering if required

Occasionally there may be a need to utilise variable attenuation within a signal circuit. A simple circuit using a single BA379 pin diode is shown. Construction must observe minimal lead lengths (as with all VHF/UHF wiring) to reduce inductive effects. In a Band 1 circuit maximum attenuation will be typically 25–30 dB and at minimum attenuation an insertion loss of 1–1.5 dB will be suffered. It is possible to series connect a 2nd BA379 diode to increase maximum attenuation figures to over 50 dB though there is a corresponding increase in the minimum attenuation insertion loss.

Constant impedance attenuators are available from aerial component stockists intended for VHF/UHF 'in-line' use. These are normally very small metal housings with integral coaxial socket/plug mating, having a typical 0–25 dB attenuation range via a screwdriver adjustment.

USEFUL TABLES AND ADDITIONAL REFERENCE MATERIAL

dB to Voltage Ratio

dB	Ratio	dB	Ratio	dB	Ratio
0	1.00	20.0	10.0	40.0	100
0.5	1.06	20.5	10.6	40.5	106
1.0	1.12	21.0	11.2	41.0	112
1.5	1.19	21.5	11.9	41.5	119
2.0	1.26	22.0	12.6	42.0	126
2.5	1.33	22.5	13.3	42.5	133
3.0	1.41	23.0	14.1	43.0	141
3.5	1.50	23.5	15.0	43.5	150
4.0	1.59	24.0	15.9	44.0	159
4.5	1.68	24.5	16.8	44.5	168
5.0	1.78	25.0	17.8	45.0	178
5.5	1.88	25.5	18.8	45.5	188
6.0	2.00	26.0	20.0	46.0	200
6.5	2.11	26.5	21.1	46.5	211
7.0	2.24	27.0	22.4	47.0	224
7.5	2.37	27.5	23.7	47.5	237
8.0	2.51	28.0	25.1	48.0	251
8.5	2.66	28.5	26.6	48.5	266
9.0	2.82	29.0	28.2	49.0	282
9.5	2.99	29.5	29.9	49.5	299
10.0	3.16	30.0	31.6	50.0	316
10.5	3.35	30.5	33.5	50.5	335
11.0	3.55	31.0	35.5	51.0	355
11.5	3.76	31.5	37.6	51.5	376
12.0	3.98	32.0	39.8	52.0	398
12.5	4.22	32.5	42.2	52.5	422
13.0	4.47	33.0	44.7	53.0	447
13.5	4.73	33.5	47.3	53.5	473
14.0	5.01	34.0	50.1	54.0	501
14.5	5.31	34.5	53.1	54.5	531
15.0	5.62	35.0	56.2	55.0	562
15.5	5.96	35.5	59.6	55.5	596
16.0	6.31	36.0	63.1	56.0	631
16.5	6.68	36.5	66.8	56.5	668
17.0	7.08	37.0	70.8	57.0	708
17.5	7.50	37.5	75.0	57.5	750
18.0	7.94	38.0	79.4	58.0	794
18.5	8.41	38.5	84.1	58.5	841
19.0	8.91	39.0	89.1	59.0	891
19.5	9.44	39.5	94.4	59.5	944
				60.0	1000

20 dB = Voltage Ratio of 10 (10^1)
40 dB = Voltage Ratio of 100 (10^2)
60 dB = Voltage Ratio of 1000 (10^3)
80 dB = Voltage Ratio of 10,000 (10^4)
100 dB = Voltage Ratio of 100,000 (10^5)
120 dB = Voltage Ratio of 1,000,000 (10^6)

dBmV Conversions to Voltage Levels

dBmV	Voltage (μV)	dBmV	Voltage (μV)	dBmV	Voltage (mV)	dBmV	Voltage (mV)
−60	1.00	−30	31.6	0	1.00	+30	31.6
−59	1.12	−29	35.5	+ 1	1.12	+31	35.5
−58	1.26	−28	39.8	+ 2	1.26	+32	39.8
−57	1.41	−27	44.7	+ 3	1.41	+33	44.7
−56	1.59	−26	50.1	+ 4	1.59	+34	50.1
−55	1.78	−25	56.2	+ 5	1.78	+35	56.2
−54	2.00	−24	63.1	+ 6	2.00	+36	63.1
−53	2.24	−23	70.8	+ 7	2.24	+37	70.8
−52	2.51	−22	79.4	+ 8	2.51	+38	79.4
−51	2.82	−21	89.1	+ 9	2.82	+39	89.1
−50	3.16	−20	100	+10	3.16	+40	100
−49	3.55	−19	112	+11	3.55	+41	112
−48	3.98	−18	126	+12	3.98	+42	126
−47	4.47	−17	141	+13	4.47	+43	141
−46	5.01	−16	159	+14	5.01	+44	159
−45	5.62	−15	178	+15	5.62	+45	178
−44	6.31	−14	200	+16	6.31	+46	200
−43	7.08	−13	224	+17	7.08	+47	224
−42	7.94	−12	251	+18	7.94	+48	251
−41	8.91	−11	282	+19	8.91	+49	282
−40	10.0	−10	316	+20	10.0	+50	316
−39	11.2	− 9	355	+21	11.2	+51	355
−38	12.6	− 8	398	+22	12.6	+52	398
−37	14.1	− 7	447	+23	14.1	+53	447
−36	15.9	− 6	501	+24	15.9	+54	501
−35	17.8	− 5	562	+25	17.8	+55	562
−34	20.0	− 4	631	+26	20.0	+56	631
−33	22.4	− 3	708	+27	22.4	+57	708
−32	25.1	− 2	794	+28	25.1	+58	794
−31	28.2	− 1	891	+29	28.2	+59	891
						+60	1.00V

LTS $= 10^{-6}$
TS $\ = 10^{-3}$

CONCLUSION

In the foregoing pages has been discussed the possibility of receiving television signals over long distances, and the resolving of such pictures hopefully with the minimum of distortion on the TV screen. It is certainly possible, and with the minimum of equipment, to receive strong signals over distances far in excess of the normal 'local' signals. A beginner to the hobby would be well advised to initially concentrate on the easier modes of propagation such as Sporadic E. This enables signals of high strength to be received over quite considerable distances and with the very basic of aerial systems — a wideband dipole feeding into a VHF Band 1 receiver sufficing. The results, hopefully spectacular, will then enthuse the viewer to quest for the more difficult forms of propagation that necessitate greater skills and improved hardware — and of course greater dedication to the hobby.

The content of this book has been compiled by an active enthusiast, and with the assistance and suggestions from other TV-DX enthusiasts, and in the hope that the accumulated information will be a practical guide for the beginner and a source of reference for the established enthusiast.

This revised and extended volume retains much of the information from earlier editions and has been supplemented with updated and new material, hopefully to make for a more comprehensive guide to this absorbing hobby, a hobby where the individual still can experiment and innovate — many of the circuits herein were devised by TV-DX enthusiasts for specific applications where no commercial product was available. A final word of warning — if construction or modification of mains operated equipment is envisaged take great care — if uncertain — don't! May you enjoy good reception.

Useful Sources for Further Reading/Reference
A full compendium of satellite footprints for Worldwide application together with downlink content detail and other technical information is contained in Steve Birkill's book *STTI's International Satellite TV Reception Guidebook* from STTI Inc., P.O. Box G, Arcadia, OK 73007, USA, telephone (405) 396-2574 at $25 US funds. VISA, ACCESS, American Express.

Booklets of UK TV/FM transmitting station detail are available from:
Engineering Information Service, IBA, Crawley Court, Winchester, Hants SO21 2QA.

BBC Engineering Publicity, Broadcasting House, London W1A 1AA.

British Amateur Television Club, c/o 'Grenehurst', Pinewood Road, High Wycombe, Bucks HP12 4DD (membership enquiries/applications).

H.S. Publications, 7 Epping Close, Mackworth Estate, Derby, DE3 4HR (DX publications).

Aerial Techniques, 11 Kent Road, Parkstone, Poole, Dorset BH12 2EH (aerial equipment and DX publications, formally known as Southwest Aerials).

When writing to BBC, IBA, BATC, HS or AT, please include a stamped self-addressed foolscap envelope.

The author of this book writes a monthly TV-DXing column, *Long Distance Television* in *Television* magazine (IPC).

TV-DXing columns also appear in *Radio and Electronics World* (REW) and *Practical Wireless.*

Earlier editions of this volume enjoyed wide distribution and although the general techniques are applicable to most parts of the World it became obvious that certain points needed expansion to foreign readers. As an example the measurements for aerials in this volume are in Imperial (i.e. feet and inches) since despite metrication within the UK, Imperial measurements are still generally used and understood by the majority in preference to the new metric standard.

Metric however is in widespread use in Europe and the following conversions should enable such readers to establish the appropriate dimensions:

1 inch = 2.54 cm	1 foot = 30.48 cm
1 cm = 0.394 inches	1 metre = 39.4 inches
1 km = 0.621 miles	

Coaxial cable is gaining in popularity due to the ease of fitting and routing. Ribbon feeder however enjoys widespread use, noteably in the Americas and Australasia. Most aerial manufacturers have available matching transformers for both VHF and UHF enabling a 75-ohm source (e.g. an aerial) to convert to 300-ohm ribbon. VHF transformers are inevitably ferrite cored devices but those for UHF may either be of ferrite or a miniature printed circuit board. The transformers are wide band in operation and have only a nominal insertion loss (typically less than 0.5 dB) provided a good quality device is employed. It is possible incidentally to obtain ferrite cored aerial combiners in certain overseas markets which allows 2 aerials to be combined/stacked without the bandwidth restriction associated with conventional cable harness. Again good quality units must be used in the interests of good matching and a low insertion loss. Certain tropical areas are prone to high level static conditions and regular thunder/lightning storms. It is advisable to avoid the use of a masthead amplifier in these areas since a close strike or gradual build-up of static within an aerial system can well mean the demise of a transistor in such an amplifier. It is a wise precaution to include static discharge paths with an aerial system/feeder such as VHF chokes to earth or high value discharge resistors (e.g. 5k ohms non-inductive). Certain masthead amplifiers will have protection diodes fitted across the input circuit to reduce the possibility of damage due to static build-up.

Voltage supplies in certain parts of the World can fluctuate considerably, if it is necessary to adjust mains tappings regularly then some means of monitoring the incoming mains should be provided (e.g. voltmeter) to avoid overdriving the components in the receiver. Transformers are available that will give a relatively constant output voltage between extremes of incoming voltage. It must again be stressed that TV receivers can be lethal and due precautions must be taken if the rear protective cover is removed.

A further danger must be stressed. In previous sections mention has been made of Sunspots. The Sun must never be viewed directly with a telescope or binoculars since serious injury to the eye will result even if viewed for an instant. Attempts at observing sunspot activity must only be made by projecting the Sun onto a white card.

APPENDIX 1

RE-ENGINEERED UK ALLOCATIONS FOR BANDS 1, 3

(Courtesy of DTI)

Frequency (MHz)

49.00   An unspecified 500 KHz to be allocated into fixed paging services at 49 MHz from 1987.

Simplex	*Duplex (where used)*	
174.00 – 174.50		Fixed communication links for emergency services (UK landbased)
174.50 – 176.50		Private mobile radio (PMR), Simplex
176.50 – 183.50	184.50 – 191.50	Private mobile radio, base transmitters
183.50 – 184.50		Private mobile radio, Simplex
184.50 – 191.50	176.50 – 183.50	Private mobile radio, mobile transmitters
191.50 – 192.50		Private mobile radio, Simplex
192.50 – 199.50	200.50 – 207.50	Private mobile radio, mobile transmitters
199.50 – 200.50		Private mobile radio, Simplex
200.50 – 207.50	192.50 – 199.50	Private mobile radio, base transmitters
207.50 – 208.50		Private mobile radio, Simplex
208.50 – 215.00	216.50 – 223.50	Private mobile radio, base transmitters
215.50 – 216.50		Private mobile radio, Simplex
216.50 – 223.50	208.50 – 215.60	Private mobile radio, mobile transmitters
223.50 – 225.00		Private mobile radio, Simplex

N.B.:   PMR to operate at 12½ KHz channelling, commercial cordless phones and data handling to be permitted.

INDEX

NOTES